P9-DFJ-976

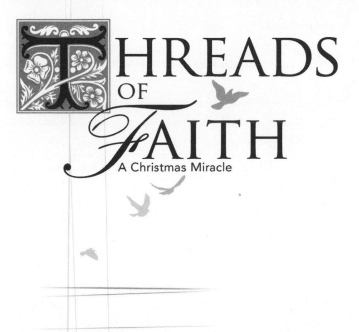

THREADS OF FAITH

A Christmas Miracle

SHAUNA V. BROWN

BONNEVILLE BOOKS
AN IMPRINT OF CEDAR FORT, INC.
SPRINGVILLE, UTAH

SPECIAL APPRECIATION

To the Brown's Sunshine Factory and those friends and pioneers who encouraged me to push forward with a dream and testimony.

© 2011 Shauna V. Brown
All rights reserved.

No part of this book may be reproduced in any form whatsoever, whether by graphic, visual, electronic, film, microfilm, tape recording, or any other means, without prior written permission of the publisher, except in the case of brief passages embodied in critical reviews and articles.

This is a work of fiction. The characters, names, incidents, places, and dialogue are products of the author's imagination, and are not to be construed as real.

ISBN 13: 978-1-59955-921-6

Published by Bonneville Books, an imprint of Cedar Fort, Inc., 2373 W. 700 S., Springville, UT 84663
Distributed by Cedar Fort, Inc., www.cedarfort.com

LIBRARY OF CONGRESS CATALOGING-IN-PUBLICATION DATA

Brown, Shauna V., 1949- author.
  Threads of faith : a Christmas miracle / Shauna V. Brown.
      p. cm.
  Summary: In England in the 1830s, a young woman joins the Church of Jesus
Christ of Latter-day Saints and faces the possibility of being disowned by
her father.
    ISBN 978-1-59955-921-6
  1. Mormon converts--England--Fiction. 2. Father and
child--England--Fiction. I. Title.
  PS3602.R72287T48 2011
  813'.6--dc22
                                        2011014692

Cover design by Brian Halley
Cover design © 2011 by Lyle Mortimer
Edited and typeset by Kelley Konzak

Printed in the United States of America

10 9 8 7 6 5 4 3 2 1

Printed on acid-free paper

PREFACE

S I stood on Rocky Ridge, dripping wet and wind whipped, I gained an insight and inspiration that would start me on a fifteen-year journey of research and study of pioneers.

Two years later, in the month of December, my stake president, Stewart Glasier, asked if I would write a stage production about the Willie and Martin Handcart Companies. Our stake youth would be experiencing a handcart trek, and he desired something to inspire as well as educate them in preparation.

"Silhouettes against the Storm" was written, music scored, and a cast of two hundred people dressed in pioneer clothing breathed life into the story. For me, it would be the beginning of a love affair with the pioneers' history. I am forever grateful for those who crossed the ocean, who were driven by the Spirit upon trails, and who willingly sacrificed for the sake of family and the gospel.

Long after the curtain closed and the applause fell silent, I continued to follow the journeys of many of the Saints. Journals and stories filled my insatiable thirst to know what made them leave their homelands and loved ones and cleave to a new religion as they traveled into the unknown. Some were abandoned or disowned and had their homes burned to the ground. Even entire towns forced some to depart because of contrary beliefs. The stories are endless, the sacrifices numerous, and their courage continues to be inspiring.

As a Christmas gift to friends and neighbors, I wrote a story—a historical work of fiction that was inspired by true events. Then, with the response and interest of many, the story grew. More facts and more impressions came to light as Hillary Whitman became the spokesperson for those who lived the story.

I believe with full heart that each of us may become the way and means for others to pursue the truth. You and I can become an instrument for good in our own right. Perhaps it will be because we felt the need to lift our voice of testimony. Perchance it will be our gift to another to motivate them to ponder, pray, and ask concerning "restored truths." Ultimately our purpose is to bring one closer to Christ.

Whether in the walk, the voyage, or the climb, it is in God's grand design for us to return and embrace in a warm and joyous reunion—to someday be surrounded by those who have gone before and to recognize that the challenges, the experiences, and the sacrifices were worth everything.

Shauna V. Brown

CHAPTER I

Home Again

December 17, 1839
Stafford, England

 LACING my luggage beneath the willows, I stood cautiously, concealed by the large birch tree, looking at the house that had been my home for fourteen years. It looked just as I imagined it would for Christmas, with holiday wreaths hung upon the door and the windows. I had always loved Christmas, and instantly I was flooded with thoughts of Christmases past. I could almost taste the fruit breads and pudding. I found myself wishing it could be as it had been before.

"Home," I whispered. Yet a sadness filled my mind as a sting of a memory remained. I could almost hear those smarting demands of my father. It seemed as fresh as if it were yesterday when he said, "Your name shall never be spoken here again."

That door, that very door now holding a holiday wreath, had been closed to me. It all happened as a result of my curiosity. I was just fourteen then. James Mooney had told my friend Sarah that some missionaries from America had been baptizing people down by Blythe Bridge. Sarah was always looking for new adventures, so she asked me to attend a Church gathering of those missionaries at the Bowmans's farmhouse.

I recall Sarah saying in a most convincing voice, "We

1

can be spies for your father, Hillary. We can tell him everything they say."

However, with a sense of fear, I countered, "But what if they find out I am the daughter of a Methodist minister?"

"We'll just stand in the back and out of sight," she insisted.

I had always wanted to go to a revival but never had the courage till then.

There was a large group of people gathered. I scanned the group to see if there was anyone I recognized, but hiding behind a large wooden beam didn't allow much access to view. On my tiptoes, I could see a small group of men standing before those gathered. They didn't look like ministers to me. My father was always dressed in his finest suit. They, in comparison, dressed so simple, much like the common man.

One of the younger men stood before us and introduced himself. "I am Elder Larson. I am sent by the Lord to share a message of eternal and everlasting truth."

I was impressed with his conviction and passion. They seemed different to me than what my father described: "Unversed, uneducated, so-called ministers of God. They come just to promote their book worth fourteen shillings."

I must admit I was confused with the whole of it. They seemed genuine. As I listened intently to Elder Larson's sermon, I forgot the intent of our secret visit. I was supposed to be spying, but as he addressed us, I was filled with interest instead. He spoke with warm confidence and conviction as he declared and testified of the principles of a newly organized gospel.

After a time, Sarah wanted to leave, and she cast a frustrated look my way. But I shook my head and indicated that I would listen a little longer.

As I listened to their message, I felt something new

within me and rejoiced as a new clarity of faith in Christ, repentance, and the gift of the Holy Ghost brought a glorious light that flooded my mind. My heart warmed to the truth of what they said. At the meeting's end, I found myself asking to borrow one of the books from the missionaries. "I must share it with my family," I insisted.

Eager to share my findings, I ran most of the way home. Breathless, my feeling of excitement tumbled forth as I dashed into my father's study and proclaimed, "I just heard a wonderful, inspired sermon. It was a message of glorious light and godly plainness. Oh, Father, you must teach it to the congregation," I pleaded. Holding up the book I borrowed, I parted the pages, "It's a Book of Mormon. I marked it here. Listen. Alma 37."

I remember being so excited to share my feelings as I read aloud, "'Let all thy thoughts be directed unto the Lord; yea, let the affections of thy heart be placed upon the Lord forever.

"'Counsel with the Lord in all thy doings, and he will direct thee for good; yea, when thou liest down at night lie down unto the Lord, that he may watch over you in your sleep; and when thou risest in the morning let thy heart be full of thanks unto God; and if ye do these things, ye shall be lifted up at the last day.'"

"Father, it's like what you teach. It's like hearing the words straight from God. Those missionaries were warm, and I feel the truth of what they were saying here within my soul. They spoke of restored truth."

Instantly my father countered, "Truth? You are but a child and think you know the truth? Those men tickle your ears with verbiage to entice you. You have been deceived, Hillary." Then he started to pepper me with questions: "Restored truth? Does that make any sense to you? How is truth restored?"

"God came down to Joseph Smith—" I began.

My father interrupted, "And you believe that God spoke with a fourteen-year-old boy? I have heard all about that Joseph Smith, the golden book, and angels. It's all the talk of late. Why, just yesterday I talked with Mr. Applebee, and he informs me that it seems anyone who walks onto the grounds of the Bowmans's farm are under some power of those Mormon preachers. And the idea of my daughter turning ear to another church . . . I can't believe it! Have you no feelings, Hillary? I have a congregation that follows me. I went to Trinity Divinity School. Where did that Joe Smith go, or his so-called Elders?"

Suddenly my face turned red hot. "Father!" I countered, "Won't you listen for a moment?"

"God picks a boy—a fourteen-year-old—to be His messenger to the world?" he said, shaking his head in disgust, his face now flushed with small beads of sweat. "How can you believe such talk? I think you believe that Joe Smith is a prophet—like Moses or Abraham. Those missionaries have caused quite a stir among our people. They are of the devil. Now let it go."

I countered once again, "Father, Sarah and I stood in the corner of the room behind a large wooden post so no one would see us. I went for you—to see and understand different beliefs and to let you know what I learned. But Father, I must tell you, it was a sermon of love. There was no pounding on a podium or crying repentance or giving speeches of fear. There was no talk of flames from hell to make one tremble. It all made me feel good inside. You should go and hear them, Father."

He moved toward me, close enough that I could feel his breath against my face.

"I can't believe it. My eldest daughter, standing there

listening to those Mormons, lured into believing their 'golden bible?'" He grabbed the book from my hands and threw it to the ground with disgust. "That is what I think of it! You can't believe that a boy talks with God in a grove of trees and then writes this book from golden plates. Joe Smith hasn't even been to school. How could he write a book, let alone lead a church? You have clearly been duped, Hillary Whitman." Turning away from me, he walked across the room and continued, "Might you recall, all we need from God is the Bible and nothing more." Then, looking at me with hot anger, he asked, "What must the people be saying of you, Hillary?" His eyes were staring directly into my face. "Forget this nonsense!"

Feeling weak in my knees and a queasiness in my stomach, I thought to run to my bedroom. Yet I felt compelled to face my father once again. "Father, for years I have heard you preach about picking up the cross and following Jesus Christ, and because I feel what the Mormon elders are teaching—"

Losing his patience with me, he interrupted, "One solitary meeting, and you've been changed in a twinkling of an eye to believe strangers. You are too young to understand. I shall not hear one more word from you this day. You will go to your room and stay in your room till you no longer have the desire to follow the winds of deception that have blown into your mind. Hillary, you will not make a mockery of my position."

Squeezing me hard by my arm, he led me to my bedroom. I felt a current of tears streaming down my cheeks. He slammed the door behind me, and I sunk to the floor beside my bed, sobbing for what seemed hours. What had I done?

Silence

Days passed, and silence hung within our home, where it was normally filled with happy conversation. Father was true to his demand for silence, and no further discussion about the Church was addressed. Nightly, a tray of food was delivered to me promptly at half past five and left beside my door. A single knock announced its arrival.

Early one morning, I could hear Lucinda humming up the steps as she approached my room. All sounds were welcome visitors.

"Here's your food: Hot porridge, soft eggs, toast, and juice," announced Lucinda, "and more."

I hurried to the door in hopes of catching a glimpse of her. I was delighted to see Lucinda standing in the corner of the hallway. No words were shared, only a smile and a blown kiss. She motioned for me to look under the napkin. Pulling back the cloth revealed a book and a letter. It was the Book of Mormon. Quickly, I covered the tray. "Hidden treasures! Thank you," I softly whispered. I slipped back into my room and closed the door behind me. Delight and fear filled my heart all at once.

Seeing the note tucked into the front cover of the book, I smiled as I recognized Lucinda's handwriting. It had been nearly two weeks—two lonely weeks. I opened the note and read:

Dearest Hillary,

I love you and miss our talks. I am scared. Father is so different. Can you please make things right with Father? Mother's heart is broken, and her eyes are puffy and swollen. She is set to crying most of the time. It is hard to live within our home where one so loved as you is treated like a prisoner. I know you can be stubborn, Hillary.

I found your Book of Mormon when I went to the trash box. I rescued it. I have been thinking, since you had such strong feelings that day within your soul, you need to find answers. Perhaps you can find them in the book. I believe you must read it. Our home is so different. I'm so afraid for you, dear sister. If you could read and study this book and save us all from this experience, I would be ever grateful.

Your loving sister,
Lucinda

"Bless you. Bless you, Lucinda," I whispered.

It wasn't long before I welcomed any form of sound or conversation. Continual silence seemed to darken my spirit. Gratefully, the kitchen was located beneath my room, and frequently I would place a glass cup to the floorboards and listen.

"It would make me crazy," said Lucinda to my mother, "locked up in that room day and night with no one to talk to. What good is it going to do?"

"I don't know. Perhaps your father just wants her to think about her beliefs, but there isn't much I can do to change your father's stand. He is set upon his word, and Hillary will stay there till she has a change of heart."

"How can Hillary change her heart?" asked Anna.

"We'd best be getting the dinner tray ready for Hillary," said Mother. "Cut her an extra large piece of spice cake. It's her favorite."

An extra large piece of cake—that was so like my mother. Even though my father was direct and insistent, she always maintained a soft, steady, caring affection.

My interest was piqued when I heard Lucinda tell Mother

that Miss Holland had asked about my school absences. "She's really worried and wants to know what Hillary has got. What do we tell her, Mother?"

Even through the floorboards I could sense Mother's frustration and concern, especially when Anna shared that Benson Willis asked if Father is going to join those Mormons.

Mother's voice instantly got loud, "Girls, this is an impossible state for all of us to be in. Sarah and Hillary's adventure has set off a flurry of debates. This foolishness is ruining many a family in Stafford. Can't you see what this has done, even to ours? Beyond that, can you imagine how difficult it is for your father? He has his own church and congregation to worry about. We must trust that God will hold us together."

I placed the glass upon my dresser. I couldn't listen any longer. To slice the spirit of sadness from my heart, I started to sing at the top of my lungs. I hoped the familiar melody would rest upon them and they would welcome my rendition of our favorite Methodist hymn:

"Oh, say but I'm glad, I'm glad.
Jesus has come and my cup runneth o'er,
Oh, say but I'm glad.
Wonderful, marvelous things he brings
into a heart that's sad,
Through darkest tunnel the soul doth sing,
Oh, say but I'm glad."

For a moment, I felt relief and renewed courage. "Father can't forbid me from singing his favorite song." And so I sang louder. Then, to my delight, I heard more voices join in singing.

"Oh, say but I'm glad . . .
Wonderful, marvelous things he brings

into a heart that's sad."

Their voices grew louder and stronger in melody, and for those few moments in song, I felt even greater love for them.

"Oh, say but I'm glad, I'm glad . . ."

✳

The days were long and always the same. I longed to talk with someone. My little glass cup had become a faithful comrade so I didn't feel so alone in the silence.

I was grateful when Mother would take to her spinning. The sound of Mother pumping the treadle was so sweetly familiar. I missed, however, the magic of watching the thin threads spin. It made me think of happier times—times when Mother would sing aloud the spinning song and we would hum or tap our shoes. I could hear her just below me, but I felt so far away.

I soon came to understand why Father had ordered silence and separation. Silence can become so deceptive to the mind. I began to doubt myself and question what I truly believed. One moment I would want to pound upon the door for freedom, and then I would be taken back to words Elder Larson had spoken. My soul was in deep conflict.

I picked up the Bible and said aloud, "Lord, help me understand."

I had, on several occasions, played a personal game of finding answers from God—directly. Closing my eyes, I thumbed the pages of the Bible. When I opened my eyes, I found myself in 2 Corinthians. I raised my finger and then dropped it onto the page. Clearly I don't believe that there are coincidences in life. It was a passage to the Corinthians, written when Paul the Apostle was in prison.

"'Therefore I take pleasure in infirmities, in reproaches,

in necessities, in persecutions, in distresses for Christ's sake: for when I am weak, then am I strong.'"

"Thank you, God. I will be strong," I said while looking out the window. Sweet emotion filled my heart as tears accompanied the moment. I felt renewed in my cause.

It was early—much too early for the breakfast tray. It was almost as though I was looking at an angel. It was my mother. In an instant, I was in her arms. She felt like Mother, dressed like Mother. It wasn't a dream.

She stood silent for a moment and then extended, "Your father feels it best for you to attend school. There has been much talk of late, and to thwart further questions, he has given you permission to go to school."

I eagerly embraced the opportunity and took my mother by the hands. Together we danced in a circle. Mother was clearly delighted by my spirit of joy.

I quickly filled the washbasin with water and washed and readied for the day. There was a sense of newness in my heart. My clothes seemed to fly onto my body. I danced down the hallway and blew kisses at the pictures on the wall. Entering the dining room, I slid into my chair at the table and winked at Lucinda. I then reached out and touched Anna's hand. Instinctively, she held mine tight.

"You may be free from your room only to attend school, and you shall not speak to anyone," my father instructed while sitting at the head of the table. I could see by the frozen look on his face that he was resolved. I felt a sense of guilt, as clearly something had changed within him.

For weeks I attended school and sat in silence. I envisioned myself a heroine, like unto Joan of Arc, standing for beliefs, defending truth at all costs. "Through pain and sorrow, I will walk tall," I often told myself. I was diligent in my school studies as well as my secret and intense study of the Book of Mormon. Then a strong desire filled me with courage. At a recess break between morning classes, I pulled Lucinda behind the large red cedar so no one would see us in conversation. It was then I broke the silence. "Lucinda, don't speak so you may continue to obey Father's demand. I thank you for saving the Book of Mormon. I have continued to read it every night. I overheard that the missionaries are staying at the Bowmans's farm still. I have jotted down some questions, and I am going to see the missionaries. I need to have answers and know for my—"

"Father will be stirred to a fit of anger, Hillary!" Lucinda blurted out. "I beg you not to cross him. He is so upset as each day he learns that another member of his congregation has left his church. The Morgan family, the Fieldings, even the Slaytons have joined themselves with the fellowship of the Latter-day Saints. Father is greatly grieved as well as angered by all of this. You don't see it because you're in your room, but I hear plenty."

"Lucinda," I insisted, "Father is not about to again venture into a conversation with me about the Church. I have questions, and I need answers. You mustn't tell anyone I'm going, not even Anna. If anyone asks concerning my whereabouts, just tell them that I am sick. Truly I am! It's not a lie! I am sick—sick at heart! And before I create anymore hurt to our family, I need to have answers."

"Hillary, if Father finds out—"

"Lucinda, as God is my witness, I have such strong feelings within my soul. I have never felt this way before. If I don't find out, it will hang forever on my mind, and if it is true, then I must do all I can to further the message of the Lord."

"Father said you are stubborn and hardheaded, Hillary, and now you are sounding as if you are."

"I may be stubborn, but I know I felt something different within me. It was burning warm, and I must know for myself the truth of it." Wrapping my arms around Lucinda, I felt as though I'd burst inside. "I love you so!" Then I quickly kissed her on her forehead, adding, "Not a word to anyone—promise?"

"I promise, Hillary, bu—"

I quickly waved and began running in the direction of the Bowmans's Farm.

*

It sounded like a clap of thunder as my father slammed the screen door. "Hillary, come here this moment!" he bellowed. His loud voice startled me, as I'm sure it did everyone in the house. Realizing I was in my bedroom, he told Lucinda, "Go fetch your sister immediately!"

In a moment, I could hear someone fumbling with the key to my door. Unlocking the door, Lucinda cautioned, "You'd better come quickly. Father seems beyond upset."

"What is he upset about? Did you say something?" I questioned.

"No."

"Did someone see me?"

"I don't know. I didn't say a word to anyone."

I quickly followed Lucinda to the dining room, where my father snapped, even before allowing me to sit, "I just talked with your teacher, Miss Holland. She stopped me as I was coming up the path. She asked how you were feeling.

That was strange because just this morning, I watched you, Lucinda, and Anna leave for school. You looked well enough, Hillary, and I noted, thankfully, you were not active in conversation with either one of them. So you see, I was surprised when Miss Holland inquired about your absence."

Instantly guilt flooded my face. I had been caught.

He continued, "I asked, 'Absent? My Hillary? What do you mean? Then Miss Holland informed me that for the past four days you have missed school. She also said that when she asked Lucinda concerning your whereabouts, her reply was, 'Hillary is ill.' But here you are, standing right before me, looking perfectly healthy. Sadly, I believe I have two daughters caught in a lie. One feigns illness so as to miss school, and the other lies for her. You must think I am a fool."

Lucinda searched my eyes and then declared, "It was not a lie, Father. Hillary is sick—sick at heart."

Giving her a cold stare, he barked, "I shall not have this deception. Not under my roof!"

Lucinda swallowed hard as if mustering courage to speak. "You would be ill too, Father, if you could not talk with your family, locked up each night, treated like an anim—"

"Enough from you. You can go to your room and sit in silence and become 'sick' as well." Lucinda instantly started to cry and ran up the wooden stairs.

"Father!" I exclaimed. "It is true I have missed school, and it was I who broke the rule of silence in the first place. I told Lucinda to tell anyone who asked about my absence that I was sick. Please do not punish her because of me. I will take any discipline you choose."

With an almost sarcastic tone, he continued, "I guess I don't need to ask you where you spent your days of schooling? Reading other texts, I'm sure." He smirked and glibly added, "Golden books, perhaps, given to you by an angel or better yet—he might have been the instructor!"

All eyes were now fixed upon my face, my features now infused with a mixture of fear and hot anger. Even before I could take a breath, he interjected, "Hillary, you are wasting your time. Believe me, angels and personal visits by God don't happen. That golden book is nonsense, and it is of the devil and shall take you down to hell forever! I threw that book away once. I'm sure you have another by now. Bring it to me. Go and fetch the book," he demanded.

I returned slowly, scanning the pages to recall as much as possible. My book had become such a friend to me. Father stood by the fireplace, stoking the embers with resolute disdain. Within moments I realized the punishment. Slowly I placed my cherished book in his large hands and stood in silence. Anna and my mother stood frozen in the doorway as he proudly tossed the book into the flames. The fire quickly licked the pages and curled them. My eyes filled with tears as I watched my book burn before my eyes. With a taste of bitterness, I softly stated, "You can't burn the truth, Father."

His hot response scared me. "I shall not have this evil spirit dwelling in my home. You must realize you cannot serve two masters. Today, you were caught in a lie. I cannot have it! I will not! I will not lose my place or standing in the church because of you. I refuse to be humiliated by your actions. From this day, you will no longer speak of the Mormons. I insist you stay in your room until you realize the deception. You won't be going to school, for clearly you need time to ponder and talk with God about this folly."

The Choice

The following Sunday, I was allowed to attend Father's church with the family. I'm sure it was with the hope that it would discourage any questions from his congregation. He gave a stirring sermon on repentance. Clearly it was meant for me and any others who might be questioning their beliefs. Upon our return home, I immediately went to my room. I could hear my family talking in the study, but it was difficult to make out the conversation. I had set myself to reading the Bible when I saw my door open. My father stood stoutly before me. Determined and direct, he began to speak.

"Well, Hillary, I see you are reading the Good Book. Perhaps by my sermon you have welcomed true light into your heart?"

I looked into his face, a face I had once respected, cherished, and felt such affection for. Yet now, I felt so distant from him. Pausing to organize my thoughts, I breathed deeply and prayed for the words to come, "For all my days, Father, you have taught me to love the Lord and seek for truth. I have no desire to cause you any grief, embarrassment, or shame. It was for you I ventured to the Bowmans's farm."

"Oh, you're blaming me now?" he asked gruffly.

"No, Father, there is no one to blame. You set me upon this venture of silence to pray, ponder, and know for myself." Holding the Bible closer, I affirmed, "I have studied the words of God."

"Hillary, this very day I spoke of repentance. It was my best sermon in months. As I was leaving, I overheard a member of my congregation say, 'Well, he should surely watch those of his own flock who have wandered into the Bowmans's pasture.' See, I cannot have this, Hillary! I will not. I need to know on which side of the fence you are standing. I cannot continue to harbor feelings and preach sermons of love and forgiveness when my home is exposed to evil ways. Today, Hillary, you must make a choice—and a careful choice. It will be between your family and that religion."

With thoughts exploding inside, I offered, "I wish that I didn't have to make that choice, Father. I feel I should read this to you." My hands began to shake as I removed the book marker and opened the Bible. "I was just reading in Matthew, 'He that loveth father or mother more than me is not worthy of me: and he that loveth son or daughter more than me is not worthy of me.'"

"Father," I continued, "I love my Savior, Jesus Christ, as I know you do. If I must make a choice, I must be true to that which I feel is growing within. I have a burning testimony of—"

"Testimony?" he asked in disbelief.

"Yes, Father." I spoke calmly as peace and confidence filled my heart. "In these weeks of forced seclusion and thinking, I have prayed often for answers. I have asked God—"

"And did the heavens open? Did an angel swoop down by your side?"

"Please, Father, do not . . . I so care about you—about all of my family. I wish you would be open—"

"Open?" he said, shaking his head. "You have left yourself open to the workings of the devil! You must answer me this moment, Hillary. Do you believe that Mormonism is . . . true?"

Looking intently into his face and steeped with emotion, I answered with a stronger resolution of my own, "Yes, and I must join myself with the membership of the Church of Jesus Christ of Latter-day Saints, for I believe it is true."

"Must? You *must* join them?" He asked aghast, adding, "Then *I* must have you pack your bag and be gone by first light."

I heard gasps from the hallway as my mother burst into the room. "William, you cannot mean that. You cannot throw out our daughter! She is but fourteen years old!"

"Oh, Clarissa, I can do anything I wish. I am the head of this home, family, and church. Hillary's fourteen years old, and so was that Joe Smith when God and angels came to reveal truths to him. He made his own way, and so can Hillary! I believe you heard her. She has chosen those Mormons." Raising his fists into the air and shaking his head, he continued, "I have encouraged her to stop this ridiculous fascination with them. She has been secluded from everything for weeks. I would have thought by now she would have realized her folly. I have taught her for fourteen years, and in a few days, she is willing to follow Joe Smith to America, to a place they call Zion." Then, looking directly at me as if he could burn a hole in my heart, he said, "Hillary says she has a testimony— testimony! I gave her a choice—her family or that church."

"But William—" my mother protested.

"Stop, Clarissa! Hillary has brought this upon herself." Then he spoke the words to me that cut so deep. "You are no longer welcome under this roof, and that is the end of it! You have chosen whom you wish to follow." Then, speaking loudly and with greater emphasis, "From now on, Hillary Whitman is dead and gone. We will never speak of her again—is that clearly understood?"

Noticing Lucinda in the hallway, my father set her to work, "Lucinda, go and secure a piece of luggage for your sister and help her pack. Hillary is to be gone by first light."

He left the room muttering something. I felt as if all the air had been sucked from my soul, so I sat wearily on my bed and watched as my mother followed quickly behind him. Then I heard the front door slam and my mother crying. Again I wondered, "What have I done?"

Lucinda obediently carried a suitcase and placed it upon my bed. Within minutes, we had my few clothes folded and packed. We were both sobered by the reality of what was happening.

"I don't want you to go," cried Lucinda.

"I don't want to go, Lucinda, but you heard Father. There is no other way. I have brought enough sorrow to him, and to you all."

"Can't you just tell him—"

"Lucinda, I cannot. For all the love I have in my heart for my family, I cannot cause my soul to deny the feelings I know to be true. God even says that if we aren't willing to leave those we love, we are not worthy of Him."

"But God does not want us unhappy. What will become of you, Hillary? What will I do without you? Where will you go?"

"I don't know. I guess I'll go and find the missionaries. I'm sure they will help me. I'll go to the Bowmans's farm first thing."

Farewell

It was in the dark of night that my mother tiptoed into my bedroom. Carefully closing the door behind her, she crawled upon my bed. I felt her arms encircle me. "Oh, Mother," I quietly cried, "what will I do without you?" I felt her tears against my cheeks.

"Are you sure, Hillary, that this is what you want to do? My heart will break, I'm sure of it."

"Please, Mother, I have cried every night for months. It will take all the courage I can muster to follow Father's demand. I know now that I must leave. I have to honor what I have found. In my quiet prison, I have found truth."

"But how do you know it is?" Mother whispered.

"Something within my soul has felt it."

"I can't believe you must leave us."

"I will always remember your love, Mother."

Tears accompanied our quiet conversation deep into the night.

With the light resting upon the willows outside the window, I knew it was time for me to leave. With my suitcase in hand, I slowly walked on the stepping-stones that led to the wooden gate. Somehow, I was more aware than ever before of the Irish moss between the stones, the clover in the thick grass, and the sparrow nestling in my mother's favorite yellow rosebush. Scanning my surroundings, my throat felt thick as I realized I might never return, and now tears were fresh upon my cheeks. Reaching for the latch on the white wooden gate, I recalled that just a few months previous, I had been careful to paint it well. Unlatching the lock, I turned and gave one last look. Standing on the porch were my two sisters and my mother. They were still, almost in statue form. I studied the picture a moment and quickly realized my father was nowhere to be seen. I then closed my eyes to solidify the memory in my mind.

"God bless you all," I said aloud, my voice trembling. "Remember I love you forever." I felt my heartstrings sever as I watched three figures in dresses embrace each other, their audible cries matching mine. I walked away quickly, not wanting them to see the increasing tears tumbling down my cheeks, and, almost in defiance of the weeks of induced silence, I yelled as loud as possible so that all within ear could hear, "I love you, I love you all forever! And I love Jesus Christ, and I will follow Him."

Then I heard a faint cry, "Oh, Hillary, what will become of you?"

CHAPTER II

New Beginnings

Sedgley, England
September 1836

HIVERING in the cold morning, Elder Smithers and I stood and watched our puffs of white breath rise magically and disappear.

"Clearly, this chill is an indication that fall is in the wings," said Elder Smithers. "We'll get warm in a few minutes. I'll knock a little harder. Did I tell you that Sister Clark is the niece of Brother Bowman? They joined the Church one year ago. Sister Clark is expecting a new wee one, which will make five children for them. With that many children, I am sure you will earn your board and keep." After pounding once again a little louder, he added, "I promise they will take good care of you. In fact, I will check on you as often as I am in Sedgley."

I smiled, "Thank you, Brother Smithers, I would welcome your visits. You have been most generous with your time and care for me."

"Listen. I hear movement," he said, putting his ear to the wooden door. "Can you smell that?" With a whiff, I was hit with a sudden hunger pang. "I bet if you are as starved as I am, you could eat—"

Just when he was about to knock again, the door quickly opened to reveal the sounds and sights of a busy home. A girl was stirring something in a large pan. A little boy was carrying some wood in a basket while another child was sweeping some ashes back into the fireplace. Instantly, I felt a rush of insecurity, and I knew what it felt like to be homesick. I grinned and nodded, pretending I was pleased to be there, yet I missed my family. It made me think of Lucinda and Anna and the many times we shared chores and laughter, and then how we cried at parting. It had been weeks since I left home, but it felt as though it had been years.

"Well, at last you're here!" said a warm and welcoming voice. "We've been all a scurry to get things ready for you. I'm Miriam Clark. Come in, come in," she eagerly directed. "You must be Elder Smithers," she said, taking his hat and muffler.

"Sister Clark, I hope we haven't come too premature. It's barely first light. Our coach arrived a bit earlier than scheduled."

"It's quite all right. As you can see, we have plenty to keep us busy. I do hope you both are hungry. We are preparing a full English breakfast for you."

"Toast and all," said the little lad grinning from behind a chair. Somehow it made me smile just looking at how a family is meant to be.

Escorting me to the center of the room, Sister Clark announced, "Children, gather close. This is Hillary Whitman. She lives down the road from Uncle Ben in Stafford." Excited eyes turned toward me. "Is she our new sister?" asked the same small boy.

"No, silly. She's a keeper for Mama," announced a girl who looked about nine or ten years old.

"Everyone here has been so excited with the news that you would be coming to stay with us. We wanted to have a warm breakfast ready for you," said Sister Clark, smiling broadly.

"We've been up for some time. I've even made dumplings," said a girl, wiping her hands on an apron. Her smile alone made me feel relief, and I breathed a peaceful sigh as I felt a sweet warmth wash away my uncertainty.

The girl added, "My uncle wrote and gave us a description of you, and well he did. You have fair skin, long, flowing, jet-black hair, eyes blue as sapphires—and they are as beautiful as he said."

By this time, the same small boy was clinging to Sister Clark's apron. "As you can see," Sister Clark said while trying to maneuver around the room, "I am perhaps the most grateful for your extra hands. Tapping her tummy, she indicated, "This babe within is kicking in eager desire of its arrival, even though it is a bit off—around Christmas." Checking the oats, Sister Clark said, "Breakfast is almost ready. Rebecca has stirred a pot full of oats, and the side pork is sizzling."

"Fresh milk and eggs too," said another voice entering the room with a large bucket of milk.

"Brother Smithers, might you pull down a couple of chairs from the post for Hillary and yourself?" asked Sister Clark, pointing to the chairs hanging on the wall. They, too, were a reminder of my home. We had chairs hanging on the dining room wall that were ever ready for visitors as well.

"Let's get seated at the table, children, and then I'll make introductions of everyone while we eat. I'm sure you are hungry," Sister Clark said. "Will you offer prayer, Brother Smithers? We haven't heard a man's voice for some time in our home."

"I would be honored to do so, Sister Clark, and to extend a blessing as well."

I watched as everyone squirmed and squeezed into their chairs and then joined hands together. The girl next to me extended her hand to mine and gave me a squeeze. I smiled at her and recognized my new beginning.

"Amen!"

Looking across the table, Sister Clark smiled and said, "I guess first you'll want to know our names. This fine, good-looking young man who just brought in the milk is the head of the home while my husband is working away up north. This is Andrew, and he is twelve."

"He looks like our father, red hair and tall like a willow," said a giggly girl teasingly.

"Yes, and she's 'Silly Millie.'" Andrew sneered across the table.

"My name is Millicent," she corrected, "and I am ten years old."

"And she never does anything wrong—she's perfect, perfect, perfect!" Andrew said in a huff.

"Andrew!" Sister Clark countered, looking down her nose with a silent, scolding stare. "Rebecca is our next child, and she just turned eight. She was baptized a member of the Church a fortnight ago."

"Hillary, you and Rebecca could have been dipped together," laughed Brother Smithers. "Perhaps Miss Rebecca is still wet behind the ears." He chuckled.

"We thought she could wait until summer to be baptized by her father in warmer weather and water, but no, Rebecca wouldn't have it. 'I'm eight and can't wait,' she said, so Elder Mitchell baptized her in Chestridge Pond. It was unseasonably cold for this time of year."

"And they both nearly drowned!" Andrew snickered. "Elder Mitchell had to dip her into the water two times, and then he had the accident."

"Accident?" I asked.

"The brethren said that my braids popped up to the surface of the pond, and then my toe came out of the water. As I was getting up the second time, I slipped on a rock, and Elder Mitchell came tumbling in on top of me. I feared that I was going to be squashed and drowned for sure."

"You're so dramatic, Rebecca," said Andrew, pretending to wipe his forehead. I could tell in that very minute that life in the Clarks's home would be a charming experience. Sister Clark, clearing her throat for attention, continued, "It was freezing cold outside. But Rebecca was bound and determined. So I tucked her braids down her dress, and then together she and Elder Mitchell cautiously ventured back. He was equally as focused to make good this baptism, as it was so cold."

"It was a miracle that there weren't inches of ice. Yet, I'm sure Rebecca would have insisted that the brethren cut a hole in it," said Andrew.

"I thought I would shiver to death or my teeth would break off. I just kept chattering." Rebecca demonstrated. "Mama made me sit by the fire after we got home, with the quilt wrapped around me and up to my nose. I drank hot peppermint tea until I went to bed. Mama was so worried I might be taken with a cold."

"Please pass the toast, Andrew," Sister Clark motioned. The introductions continued around the table. "Next to Rebecca, sitting on the stool, is Jeremiah. He's four years old. He's our youngest at the moment. He loves music and gives the warmest of hugs."

Andrew eagerly interjected, "He may look little, but he's tough. He can carry a full armful of wood, and when we play stick pull—sometimes he wins."

"Yes, Jeremiah is strong!" said Millicent as Jeremiah smiled in big-boy agreement.

"We had another brother, Martin George, but he died," said Rebecca almost matter-of-factly. "Martin would be six years old this month . . ."

"But he got the fever," said Andrew.

"And passed away," said Sister Clark quietly.

I watched as Sister Clark sought to break her serious thought and patted her tummy. "If it is a boy, we will call him Stephen Joseph. If it's a girl, we'll name her Effie Lee, after my mother. It's just a matter of time before we will know."

Elder Smithers said, "Having newborn children brings a sense of wonder into a home. Those were exciting times, I'll tell you."

"How many children might you have, Elder Smithers?" inquired Sister Clark.

"Well, we have had ten, eight living—two of ours have passed as well. So I, too, have a tender spot in my heart for those who now live with God."

"So, Jeremiah," I asked, "Do you think it is a boy or a girl?" Jeremiah smiled shyly and looked down at his bowl of oatmeal.

"Jeremiah is a bit on the shy side, but he'll warm up to you, Hillary," said Rebecca.

"So to change the topic," Elder Smithers continued, "your Uncle Ben said that your husband was looking for more work and that is why you have extended a welcome to a helper."

"Yes, thank heavens. Timothy, my husband, has secured work up north in Durham in the iron mines. We are hopeful to earn enough money for all of us to travel to America someday."

"Just like me," I announced. "To be with the Saints."

"Hopefully we will help you realize it," said Sister Clark.

"Maybe we'll all go together," chirped Millicent.

"Well, until that time, welcome to our home." Then, clapping her hands together, Sister Clark announced, "I'm hungry, so I'm going to eat this English breakfast before it all gets cold."

While I stirred my oatmeal and watched the steam drift upward, my thoughts were drawn to my own home and family. I drew my finger across the table, studying the oak pattern. It looked and felt much the same as the oak table in my home, so many miles away. I could envision my own family, busy with morning chores and preparations. Mother would be cracking the eggs and Lucinda would be slicing the bread. Anna would be placing the silverware and platters on the table. It would be noisy as well, yet wonderful. It had been eight weeks since I had last seen them—eight long weeks.

"Hillary, do you want some strawberry jelly on your toast?" asked Andrew, breaking the journey of my mind.

"Oh, yes, thank you." I smiled, taking the jar. "I love strawberries." Spreading a thick red layer upon my toast, I declared, "Mother and I canned twenty-six jars of strawberries from our garden this past season, and we jarred fifteen pints of marmalade jam as well."

"Canning too?" Sister Clark marveled. "My uncle wrote that you are quite accomplished in home duties and chores."

"Yes, my parents feel it is important to be skilled in many things. I play the mandolin and the piano, and I stitch too. My mother is skilled at the spinning wheel and loom, and I have been a spinster since I was ten. I can make candles and soap, and I bake. I can read and write, and I was fortunate to have been able to go to school. My father insisted that 'knowledge is the key to heaven's gate.'"

Millicent then blurted out, to the instant shock of all, "Then why did he kick you out of your house?"

Instantly all eyes were upon me. I felt a mixture of pressing emotions, and I was grateful when Elder Smithers came to my rescue. "Hillary's father is a Methodist minister and—"

"Let's just say, he couldn't allow me to live there any longer." My voice cracked as the reality of the words struck me.

Sister Clark, obviously embarrassed, responded, "Hillary, you'll have to forgive—"

"No, no. It's all right," I countered. "I'd better get used to it. I will tell you all about it someday." I then took a large bite of toast to relieve me of any further conversation.

"It sounds as though you can do just about anything, Hillary. Have you been taught how to braid and coil hair?" asked Millicent.

"Oh, yes," I said, eying her long, auburn locks. "Perhaps you will let me comb your hair. It's the color of my little sister Anna's. I used to brush and braid it for Mother."

"Can you do mine too?" asked Rebecca. "I love braids and twists."

"Brother Smithers, is there something more I can pass your way?" asked Sister Clark.

"No, I think I feel plump as a plum and content enough I could doze a bit. It was delicious. I can't recall enjoying a breakfast quite as much. I feel confident that I have left Hillary in good hands. I believe she will be a good fit for this family," he said with a wink my way.

Rhythm to the Morning

To my surprise, Andrew woke me early one morning. "Hillary, Hillary!" he said, tugging at my shoulder. "Mother says you need to learn to milk the cow." I quickly drew the blanket over my face to block the light from his lantern.

"It's too early for anything," I offered, squinting my eyes in the darkness.

"You need to milk the cow, and you'd best hurry. Ruby milks at first light."

"Who milks?"

"You milk the cow!"

"Me, why me?" I yawned and winced. "Your mother has never said anything to me about milking a cow. I do chores in the house."

"Mother said—it's time to milk the cow."

"I don't know anything about cows or how to milk them."

"You've got to get up, Hillary. I'll be in the barn waiting."

Wiping the sleepy sand from my eyes, I quickly pulled my blouse over my nightgown and rushed to the barn.

Andrew promptly announced, "Here she is—Ruby, our cow. And she's the best milking cow we've ever had."

Eying the size of the cow, I affirmed, "She's huge. I've never touched a cow before."

"How did you get your milk?"

"Our neighbors, the Cowans, provided our family with all the milk and cream we ever needed. My father said it's how they paid their offerings." I could sense my cowardice growing in my chest, and I hesitated to get closer. "Andrew, I don't know . . ."

"The Cowans? That's funny! You got your milk from the *Cow*ans." Andrew laughed aloud.

"It's too early for jokes, Andrew. What time is it, anyway? It's clearly still nighttime black."

"Don't know, but when the rooster crows, it's time to be up." Noticing my sleepy face, Andrew nudged me hard on my shoulder. It was a touch irritating as he said, "Aw, Hillary, you'll get used to it. You'll find that milking brings a rhythm to the morning."

"Rhythm to the morning?" It was much too early to

understand that thought, but I pondered it for a few moments. Then Andrew set a strange, three-legged stool before me and said, "Here. Sit down."

"What is it?"

"A milking stool."

"I don't understand. It's only got three legs."

"It's so you can get closer to the udders and under the cow."

"I don't want to go under the cow," I yelped.

"Hillary, you have to get close enough to milk her, and we use this stool to do it. So you have to learn."

Gathering up my nightgown, I tucked it between my legs and tried to balance upon the stool. I wobbled and rocked and found myself on the barn floor. "This isn't easy, Andrew." I could see he totally understood my plight, but he also enjoyed watching me flounder.

"You'll get the hang of it, Hillary—eventually." He grinned. Soon hay was stuck to my clothes and hair.

"Ruby, she'll get it soon." he said, comforting the cow. "We just have to be a little patient."

I squared myself and squatted atop the stool, and soon I figured I had conquered it. "There, now what do I do?" I asked, trying to hold my balance at all costs. I was now facing Ruby eye to eye. "Her eyes are gigantic. They must be at least five times bigger than mine! And her breath is something—" She clearly understood every word I said as she nosed forward into my face. "Ugh!" I squirmed. "Disgusting!" Then she drizzled something awful on my cheek. I yelped and once again found myself on the ground. I quickly wiped my face with my sleeve and determined I would show her.

"Come on, Ruby. Be nice," cautioned Andrew. "Hillary, just remember, Ruby is in charge here. She's bigger than the two of us, and you need to know that. You might try to rub her here just above her nostril. She likes it."

I bravely offered "Nice Ruby" as I touched her on the spot of white above her nose. "Andrew says that I'm going to learn to milk you," I said hesitantly.

Picking up the stool, Andrew quickly sat down beside Ruby. Then he started to demonstrate. "Be sure to place the stool at a right angle to old Ruby, and sit with your head resting on her flank like this. Ruby likes routine. It makes her comfortable. If Ruby is comfortable, then she gives more milk. Hillary, there is something you must remember. Cows have to be milked at the same time each and every day— morning and evening. If you don't milk her on schedule, she'll dry up."

"Dry up? Andrew Clark, you're pulling my leg!" I said in disbelief.

"Nope, it's true. She'll dry up, and we won't have any more milk. We can't afford to lose her." Andrew reached beneath the cow and took hold of what he called an udder. Then he made me take hold of two of them.

"Squishy," I said with a hint of distress.

"It's really quite simple to milk a cow. You just have to practice. First you need to wash the udder with warm water and wipe it with a clean cloth. Then soften them by rolling them with your fingers."

"Eew! Does it hurt her?" I winced.

"No, silly, I don't think so," he said. "Then you squeeze the milk into the bucket. It's pretty simple." Within a matter of moments, Andrew was squirting milk into the bucket.

"Now you try it," he said.

I wrapped my fingers around the udder and started to pull as Andrew had shown me. At first the milk didn't come, and I tried again, and then again, and again. Finally, I squealed with joy when I saw my first stream of—

"Milk! I did it, I did it!"

"If you do it right, you'll hear the music," Andrew said. "Squeeze and squeeze again, Ruby will be your friend," he sang aloud.

I smiled at Andrew and realized I had just learned something new. After a few minutes of listening to him sing and feeling the routine of squeezing, I said, "I understand what the 'rhythm to the morning' is. It's the music of milk squirting against the side of the bucket, huh?"

"You're a quick one, Hillary Whitman," he said, patting Ruby gently on the side.

"Oh, if only Lucinda could see me milking a cow," I mused. "She would scream, I'm sure, and Anna would be terrified with the whole of it." I laughed out loud. "I never dreamed I would be milking a cow, but then I never dreamed I would be here either. I just wish I could tell my sisters."

"I bet you miss your sisters, and they must miss you as well." Andrew sensitively stated.

"Oh, yes. Just last night as I was braiding Rebecca's hair, it took me back to the countless times I would brush and brush Anna's hair. They both have beautiful and long, shiny hair. If my sisters think of me as much as I think of them, I know they must surely miss me. I just try to fill my thoughts with happy memories and keep myself busy."

"Just add milking Ruby to the list," he giggled. "Oh, I nearly forgot, when you were away helping at the Martins', Mother got a post from our Uncle Ben. He is hoping that you are doing well and sends his best. He mentioned that your father has been sharing some stirring sermons to his congregation lately. He is taking to burning copies of the Book of Mormon, saying that anyone who reads it will burn in hell."

"Burn in hell?" I abruptly stopped milking. The news was most upsetting to me. "Andrew, my father is a good man, and I love him dearly." Tears mixed with my emotions. "But at one point, we didn't see eye to eye. It's hard to think or talk about it. I know I must have broken my family's hearts."

Andrew interrupted, "So when Millicent said you were kicked out of your home, she was right?"

"I'm afraid so. Father gave me a choice: 'Choose your family or that church.'"

"You chose the Church," he said softly.

"Yes. As I was preparing to leave home, I asked if I might have a picture of my family. Father said to me, 'Once you had a family, but not now. There is no need for a picture. Our Hillary is dead.'"

"That's horrible! Couldn't anybody stop him?" Andrew questioned.

"Mother tried. She cried and begged, but my father warned her that by English law he could put them all out on the street if they didn't abide by his wishes. I know something inside of him just cracked. My interest and belief in the Mormon Church made it impossible to remain there any longer."

"What was it like when you left? Did he yell at you?"

"No, that morning as I turned to wave good-bye, there on the porch were my mother and my sisters. I looked at all the windows, but I couldn't see my father anywhere."

Silence filled the barn, and neither Andrew nor I spoke for some time. Then, breathing deeply, I began to pull on the udders again. "I need to make some music." Instant relief came as I heard the stream of milk hit the side of the bucket. Yet tears continued to roll down my cheeks.

Andrew stood, looking intently at my face, and said softly, "Hillary, thank you for sharing your story with me. It must have taken so much courage for you to leave your family that you love. Can I ask you something else?" He asked, stepping closer. "Did people poke fun at you for what you believed?"

"Oh, Andrew, yes." I was about to continue and relate an experience, but looking into Andrew's face, I sensed he was having his own struggles. "Are people making fun of you?" I asked.

Andrew looked as if he wanted to speak, but he shook his head instead.

"Tell me, Andrew."

He hesitated for a moment.

"Andrew Clark, you need to tell me about it."

"It's nothing big like yours, Hillary. I was in town picking up salt from the store. Robert Hampton yelled out to me, 'Hey, Andrew! Is it true you've got a gold Bible? How much did it cost? Do they sell them in the store?' I felt weird inside. I looked around at who might be listening. I didn't know what to do."

"Andrew, what did Jesus do," I asked, "when people mocked Him?"

"I think He just listened and didn't say anything."

"Your Uncle Ben told me, 'There will be those who mock, beat, and make afraid, but with God standing by your side, there is power.'" I looked into his face and could see he understood.

Then he added, "I guess I just needed to hear that the gospel is all worth it. I mean, you even left your family for the sake of it."

"And the Lord brought me to another home. You know, Andrew, I have two sisters, and I always wanted a brother." A grin erupted on his face as he turned red from his chin to his forehead.

Surprised, Andrew yelled out, "Hold on, Hillary, you're almost to the top of the bucket. Ruby has never filled a bucket as long as I have known her."

I smiled with pride. "Well, I guess I made a rather good rhythm this morning."

Love Heals

Months passed, and I found that despite the long hours of daily chores, there came an abundance of happy moments within the Clark home. I even came to appreciate rising early in the morning and milking Ruby on occasion. I learned to enjoy making a rhythm to the day. Milking would often lead my thoughts to memories of my home and family. Frequently I would recall the sounds of my mother singing. She was my rhythm to the day then, as she pushed upon the pedals of the old wooden spinning wheel or kneaded the dough for the bread. Oh, how I missed those melodies.

With each passing week, I marveled as I began to feel like a member of the Clark household. Each night we would gather round the table, and by the light of the fire and lanterns, we would read stories. Sister Clark had been given *The Pickwick Papers* by Charles Dickens. We delighted as we read at least eight pages each night. We were taken into adventures and wonderful stories that made the characters come to life. Oh, how we loved to hear Sister Clark read. She could make her voice change for each person. One moment she was a gruff lawyer and the next a poor widow. It wasn't difficult to see why Rebecca took to drama so naturally.

I found it interesting teaching the girls how to knit. Sometimes I wasn't the least bit patient. I hated unraveling a row or having to go and pick up a forgotten stitch. Often it would make me think of my mother, who would sit by my side and patiently watch as my hands became skilled. I kept trying to recall how I had learned. Some days I just wanted to feel my mother's hands upon mine, instructing me again. We decided that Millicent would knit a baby blanket for her first project. I hoped it would be simple enough. Hearing that the girls were learning how to knit, Mrs. Mendenhall, our next-door neighbor, gave us some leftover yarn. With all the knitting she did, I thought she could teach the girls better than I could, but Millicent insisted that I be her teacher. Each day, row after row, we watched the baby blanket grow, and as it did, our eager anticipation of placing the wee one within it grew as well. "Let's call it the happy blanket," Millicent said proudly. "I love all the colors of it."

Of course, I spent time braiding and rolling hair and tying them with ribbons. Rebecca loved the "Swiss rolls," as I called them. It reminded me of the days when Lucinda and I pretended that we were Victorian royalty. We took some handkerchiefs and danced around the room. Here, Andrew always played the part of a prince, and Jeremiah would be our court runner. Sister Clark was our attentive audience, and she always laughed with approval.

Sitting around the table one night, I taught the others some songs my mother had taught me. It didn't take long before they were singing my favorite Methodist hymn.

> *Oh, say but I'm glad, I'm glad.*
> *Oh, say but I'm glad.*
> *Jesus has come and my cup runneth o'er*
> *Oh, say but I'm glad.*

It had a lilting melody that naturally made us smile.

Andrew suggested, "Let's sing it like we are from Germany, singing in one of the pubs." He demonstrated as if holding a drinking stein in his hands. We all giggled and joined in with his antics.

Music always seems to make my soul lighter. It was so comical to gather round and lift our hands with invisible mugs and sing with full voices, sometimes as loud as we could. I'm sure the neighbors wondered what in the world we were so glad about. It still makes me smile just thinking of it.

Probably the most cherished times were at the close of day when Sister Clark would calm us all down and read from the Book of Mormon. I had my own copy then and would carefully underline my favorite scriptures. Sometimes we would pretend to be different characters from the book. Andrew really got theatrical when he played the part of Abinadi. Young Jeremiah was a wicked priest and pretended to burn him at the stake.

Then Millicent said, "Hillary is like Abinadi. She is willing to stand for what she believes, even if she loses her whole family." Pride and sadness swelled within me at the same time, and tears sprang to my eyes.

"We're your family now," said Millicent, placing her arm around my shoulder. I quickly threw my arms around her neck and embraced her.

"Yes, you are," I agreed. Then all at once everyone was in a great circle sharing hugs and embraces while laughter mixed with tears.

Morning Surprise

I was surprised and unprepared when Rebecca burst into my room early one morning. "It's time to get up, Hillary!"

I pulled the blanket up over my head as I heard her insist, "Mother says you have to go to Ruby to get the morning milk."

"It's too early, and it's Andrew's day to do it!" I turned over and mumbled something like, "Get Andrew to milk Ruby. I need . . . sleep."

She shook me hard, "Hillary, you've got to get up now. Mother said we need some milk to drink with your . . . birthday cake!" she yelled. Rebecca was instantly joined with a chorus of "Happy birthday, Hillary!" Then all I could hear were squeals, the ringing of bells, rattles, and what seemed to be at least ten people dancing around my bed. Their shadows made spooky caricatures upon the wall. Andrew held the lantern as Sister Clark held up a cake, dripping with chocolate brown frosting. She started to sing, "Happy birthday to you, happy birthday to you . . ." I sat tall in my bed, amazed that everyone was wide awake and dressed.

"Hurry to the barn!" Andrew yelled. As quickly as they arrived, they all disappeared. I found myself in silent darkness. I lit my lantern, quickly dressed, and, as directed, made my way to the awaiting group. The barn was bright with lantern light. Andrew was sitting on the stool, and Ruby seemed a bit agitated with the number of morning visitors. It seemed strange to me that a family would all be gathered around a cow. I was soon to discover a Clark family birthday tradition.

"Sit on this bale of hay and open your mouth," said Millicent, directing me to the hay bale. "It's fun and won't hurt you a bit."

That made me nervous. "What are we doing?" I questioned.

"Oh, it's a tradition Grandfather Gilbert started years ago. We do it for everyone's birthday. Cake and cream—it makes you scream," yelled Millicent, amused.

Draping a towel around my shoulders, Sister Clark raised her voice, "Ready, aim . . ."

I squinted my eyes, trying to understand what was going to happen. Then I felt something warm and wet hit my face.

"Milk!" I squealed.

"Open your mouth wide, Hillary. Andrew is going to

give you fresh cream to go along with your birthday cake," Rebecca snickered. "A squirt for every year."

"Fifteen squirts?" I asked, surprised. "I'll drown."

"Hurry and open," Millicent instructed.

There is nothing in the world like warm milk in the face to set the morning. Andrew was pretty good at shooting a stream of milk across the room, but I believe there were a few missed ones on purpose. Giggles of joy and delight caused me to finally question, "Each of you willingly goes through this tradition every year on your birthday?"

Finally, after fifteen successfully completed shots, I was allowed to wipe my face. I smiled and acted appreciative of the celebration but then affirmed to all, "Your Grandfather Gilbert must have been one strange man."

Jeremiah yelled, "Cake now!" and headed for the house. Carrying lanterns, I followed the parade.

"Get the plates out and light the candles on the cake," said Sister Clark.

"Cake for breakfast?" I asked.

"It's part of the birthday fun. I've already whipped the cream."

Andrew carried the cake slowly, with candles flickering. I was happy that they cared so much. "I can't believe it. Chocolate cake is my favorite." My mind drew quickly to my memory of one year ago. Lucinda had made me a German chocolate layer cake last year. Candles were flickering just the same. I wondered if my real family would think of me today.

"Make a wish, and it will come true," said Rebecca. All of a sudden, tears began to fill my eyes. I tried desperately to keep them back but couldn't stop the flow. I had a wish, a wonderful wish, and that would be just between God and me. I closed my eyes and tucked within my heart a dream, and then I blew the candles out.

For months I had thought about writing a letter home, but because of the last disapproving look of my father, I cowered at the thought for fear he would simply tear it up. Sister Clark must have sensed my feelings because for my birthday, she gave me a box of stationery. I thought perhaps it was an answer to my prayer. Finally, I sat down with pen in hand and determined that I would write a letter to my family. Millicent and I decided it was best to disguise it. Millicent, with her best penmanship, addressed the envelope to Lucinda Whitman. Then we heated up the sealing wax and used the family seal with the letter "C" upon it.

"Your father won't find out," smiled Millicent. "I'm sure we will outsmart him."

"I pray you are right."

I had so many things I wanted to say, so much to share about my experiences with the Clark family. But most of all I wanted my family to know that I continued to think of them and pray for them daily—that I loved and missed them. I felt a surge of hope and strength run through my soul as I concluded the note: "With fondest affection, your loving daughter." In large letters, I printed my name.

HILLARY WHITMAN, Forever.

CHAPTER III

Prayer within the Pages

THOUGHT frequently about the letter that I had sent home. I prayed with all my heart that somehow my letter would be received with love. I felt like a spy sending secret information into enemy territory.

Two weeks to the day that I sent my letter, a letter arrived for me. Looking at the envelope I could tell it was from my mother. Her handwriting was so beautiful, so pleasing to the eye. Many people paid Mother to address their invitations to special events. I traced my name with my fingertip, sensing that it had only been written a few days prior. "Oh, Mother, I miss you so." I hesitated for a moment, concerned what the letter might hold. Could she have sided with Father? Does she have bitterness within her heart? Perhaps she doesn't ever want to hear from me. Might my letter have touched her heart with understanding?

Sister Clark stood quietly by my side. Seeing my courage waver, she said reassuringly, "It will be all right, Hillary. You said a prayer when you sent your letter, and it is now in God's hands."

Taking courage, I slid my finger beneath the wax seal. "I wonder if Anna melted the wax for Mother. Often Mother would let us take turns in sealing letters. Just looking at the letter gives me a thousand sweet memories of her. Oh, and smell that!" I said excitedly, holding the letter toward Miriam. "Violets! It's her favorite perfume. My father got it from France." The fragrance gave me courage that the contents would be filled with love, so I opened the letter and read:

Dearest Hillary,

"That's good." Miriam grinned. "'Dearest' is good." Then, stepping away, she said, "I'll be quiet and let you read."

I was so surprised, Hillary, when the postman delivered your letter. The seal with the C stamp set me to wondering who was writing to Lucinda. The postman even inquired as to whom we knew in Sedgley. I didn't know anyone and merely brushed it off saying, "Oh, must be a relative or old member of the church." My interest got the best of me, and, in spite of the guilt of opening a letter addressed to Lucinda, I eagerly slid my finger under the seal.

I recognized your writing almost instantly. It took my breath away, and as I read, my tears began to fall. Oh, Hillary, how my heart longs to hear your voice and to see you again.

But as soon as I had begun, I heard your father call to me. Fear rushed up my spine. I quickly hid your letter beneath a scarf in your dresser drawer and ran down the stairs. You have no idea how much I wanted to read it. I was excited when your father shared that he would be visiting with the Wilburg family that evening. Evidently Andrew Wilburg has also taken to the words of the Mormon missionaries. Your father was going there in hopes of thwarting any attempt of 'those missionaries to steal another member away' from his congregation. I knew with your father gone, I could enjoy your letter in peace.

I watched as he drove the buggy down Aldon Avenue. I ran back to the room to secure your letter. I felt so selfish. Your sisters would have relished listening to your words, but they were away at the Bremmers's practicing a duet to sing at church on Sunday, and I just couldn't wait.

I was so focused upon reading I didn't even hear them enter the house upon their return. They finally yelled to me, "Mother, Mother!" Upon hearing their voices, I slipped the letter into my apron pocket and planned a surprise. I delighted at the thought that I would read the letter while we enjoyed some hot chocolate.

"Guess what I have in my apron pocket?" I was so excited that I couldn't even wait for them to give an answer. I gingerly rendered, "It's a letter from Hillary!"

You should have seen their faces. It was as if they hadn't eaten for weeks. Indeed, we were starved to hear from you. Your sisters looked like little baby robins waiting for the worm. I began reading the letter, but my hands were trembling and my voice was filled with tears of emotion. When you wrote, "There isn't a day that I don't pray for you," I thought of the constant prayers that I have offered in your behalf, my sweet daughter.

Before we could finish the letter, we were sadly taken by surprise. Your father returned home earlier than expected. None of us heard him enter the house. He had overheard me reading the letter. Within a matter of moments, he had torn your letter into pieces and thrown it to the floor. I felt as though life had been drained from my soul. He then went on a tirade of words, indicating that you had been beguiled and led away by the Mormons and that one by one his congregation is being stolen away. On and on he went. He was distraught and once again warned, "If you recall my words, there is no Hillary Whitman! Believe me, I am intent to see that no one derides my calling." He then reminded us that by English law, as head of this home, he could do whatever he wished.

I couldn't contain myself. My anger began to grow hot, so without even one word further, I turned and left the house.

Lucinda gathered up the pieces and tried to glue the letter together, but it was impossible. However, God granted us a small blessing. Still within my pocket was the envelope with your address. Just know, dearest daughter, that we love you.

Your Mother

My heart hugged the thoughts. I could envision Lucinda picking up the pieces of the letter from the floor, and probably in secret did she try to put the paper puzzle together. I well understood the desire to piece together a family. Looking at my surprise letter, I felt so blessed. Reading Mother's words and smelling the fragrance was to me a sweet and tender mercy. I wept as I read it over and over again. To me, it was more than a small blessing. Reading the words "Just know, dearest daughter, that we love you" was like a melody to my soul.

Hold Onto Heaven

"Oh, my goodness, Hillary! I believe that my water just broke, and I'm having some sharp pains."

Worried, I rushed to Sister Clark's side, "It's too early, isn't it? I thought you said the baby wasn't coming till Christmas."

"Well, I guess when heaven is ready, we have to be ready," she said, wincing in pain and holding her belly tight.

Fear ripped through my mind. If I thought milking a cow was scary, the idea of birthing a baby was totally beyond my comprehension.

"I haven't seen a baby born! I—"

"That is why I want you to run to Mrs. Bottoms and tell her it is time. She's delivered a good hundred babies, Hillary."

"Lie on the bed," I said. "Hold that baby in there!"

"Hurry, please!" she said, breathing hard.

Quickly grabbing a wrap, I sprung into action and gave out directions to the children. "Stay in the house, get some clean blankets, and be good. Your mother's having the baby."

I could hardly catch my breath as I ran the near quarter of a mile to Mrs. Bottoms's house.

"Mrs. Bottoms! Mrs. Bottoms! The baby is coming!" I screamed and pounded on the door. "Mrs. Bottoms! Mrs. Bottoms! You've got to be here!" I yelled while knocking even harder on the wooden door. Getting no response, I ran around the cottage to see if she might be in the barn. There was no sign of her. Then I began talking to myself, almost reassuring myself. "She'll be here any time. Give yourself a few minutes. Maybe she went to market." I nervously tapped my shoes on her wooden porch. "Where are you?" I tried to sing, but fear doesn't mix well with patience, and I found myself running down the path to the street front. There was no sign of her. Then remembering the note box by the front door, I rushed to leave a message. It was then I saw a note tacked to the frame.

Delivering Baby for the Masons.

"Masons." I sighed. "They live a good two miles away." I couldn't chance to leave Sister Clark alone for so long. The reality that I might be delivering the baby left me weak in the knees. "Oh, no!" Quickly taking a slip of paper from the message box, I jotted a note: "Baby coming at the Clark home. Urgent—Mrs. Clark in pain!" Sticking the note on the nail used for such purposes, I started my trek back. I sent a quick prayer into the heavens. "Please, Lord, send Mrs. Bottoms to us! I've never birthed a baby." My mind flashed with all the possibilities. Anxiety fanned my fear as my breathing and pace increased. "Heavenly Father, are you listening?" I continued to plead unrelentingly, "Oh, Father in Heaven, please . . . Can you please hold on to that little one till I get there? Please! Please! I don't know how to birth a baby!" Then almost in answer came the arrival of snow. "Snow? Not now! I don't have time for snow." Looking directly into heaven I continued even louder, "Are you listening, God? Hold on, heaven, till I get there!"

Rushing into the house, I quickly noted that Andrew had a basin filled with warm water on the stove, and Millicent had gathered up the muslin as ordered by her mother and was warming it by the fireplace.

"Mrs. Bottoms isn't to be found. Sister Clark, what can I do? Where shall I go? What do I need? I've never even seen a baby born, not even my sisters."

Seeing my fear as well as concern, Sister Clark calmly said, "Hillary, calm down. Everything will be all right. Everything will be fine. Be calm. Don't fear."

Shaking my head with a sense of confidence, "Yes, you should know—you've had children before. What am I worried about? You probably know what to do. I found a note. It said that Mrs. Bottoms is at the Masons. I don't have any idea how long she'll be, but I left a note telling her to come quick and that you are in pain—awful pain."

"Hillary, we just need to trust in God. He knows the timing of all things." She gave me a reassuring smile. "Say a prayer, will you, Hillary?" I could tell that Sister Clark was trying to hold back her worry. Her breathing was definitely harder, and the perspiration was beginning to bead up on her face.

I quickly requested, "Hurry, everyone, to your knees, please. We need to say a prayer. We need to pray that Mrs. Bottoms gets here presently." After gathering everyone around the bed, I started to offer up an urgent plea. "Oh, Father, I know nothing about birthing a baby, and we need your help! Please send Mrs. Bottoms here or send angels to guide me and tell me what to do . . . Amen."

With obvious nervousness in my voice, I asked, "Sister Clark, what does a midwife do?"

"Mrs. Bottoms tries to keep me calm and keep me breathing steady."

"Oh, keep you breathing steady. I can do that." I started to demonstrate, breathing in through my nose and blowing out my mouth: "In, out, in, out." Witnessing such intensity from me, a smile formed on Sister Clark's face. "Hillary, slow down. You won't be of any help if you faint."

"How long has it been?" asked Sister Clark, panting intensely. "The pain is much harder than I remember it ever being."

I fell to my knees to pray again, causing Miriam to smile, "You are going to wear out your knees, Hillary. I think you have offered at least a dozen prayers within this very hour. I think God is most mindful of us."

One more hour passed, and I remained by the bed, watching as Miriam's breathing became more labored and her pain more intense.

"Please, dear Lord, bring Mrs. Bottoms here. We need her help!" No sooner had I said those words than the door swung open, revealing Mrs. Bottoms, covered in snow.

"Hallelujah!" I squealed. "I didn't know if you would make it here in time. I had visions that I might have to bring a baby into the world all alone." Feelings of fear were quickly dispelled as Mrs. Bottoms patted my hand. "Thank you, girl. I'll take over now."

"You are an angel, Mrs. Bottoms, a true angel," I said, taking her coat and scarf to hang up. Looking heavenward, I exclaimed aloud with relief, "Thank you, God!"

Mrs. Bottoms began rubbing her hands together as she blew her breath against her fingers. "It's mighty cold out there. I believe, with just one large gust of wind, it blew me right to your front door, near a quarter of a mile!" she said, winking at Jeremiah.

"Yes, thank heavens you're here, Mrs. Bottoms," said Miriam softly. "This little one has . . . already but . . . worn me . . . out. I've been breathing . . . my . . . best but . . . the pain . . . is getting so intense . . ."

Within moments, the household was set into a busy whirl as Mrs. Bottoms assigned duties to everyone. "Andrew boy, make sure the house is warm. Keep the fire burning. Millicent, get me a cloth or something to quickly warm my hands with. Hillary, come with a clean sheet and wipe Miriam's face. She's dripping with perspiration. Children, your mother needs to be totally focused on bringing this babe into the world. She's tired and has been working hard already. We all have a grand task to do here." Looking seriously at the small group gathered, she said firmly, "I can't be pestered, bothered, or concerned for any of you. You can't get in the way or make a lot of noise. We're going to be reaching into heaven for this baby." Then, rolling up her sleeves and wrapping a kerchief around her head, Mrs. Bottoms stood in the doorway and whispered, "Pray that we can get this baby here soon!"

"Pray some more?" Andrew sputtered. "We've been praying all day."

As directed, we all flew into action following the directions of Mrs. Bottoms. Then I rested for a minute with Jeremiah and Millicent playing a game of Quartettes. However, I found it difficult to focus on matching cards, as I could only think about Miriam and the pain she must be experiencing. So, almost like the ticking of the clock, I found myself saying little prayers in order to calm my fears.

When the bedroom door opened suddenly, we all gave our instant attention.

"I could use a glass of water in here," said Mrs. Bottoms. Rebecca popped up from the table and rushed to the cupboard. "I'll get it for you."

Looking at us gathered, Mrs. Bottoms took a deep breath and said, "By the looks on your faces, you could use a good dose of distraction. The snow outside is inviting. Perhaps, Hillary, you might take the children and play for a while. I'm sure you're all feeling a bit cooped up in here just waiting." Then, pulling me aside, she said with a serious tone, "Hillary, I might have to try a few things in order to get this baby here. Better for them to be outside so they can't hear."

Within minutes, all of us were dressed in our heavy winter clothing and energetically rushing for the front door. Sticking out his tongue to catch a floating snowflake, Jeremiah giggled and said, "It kissed my nose." We all winced and winked as the flakes fluttered into our faces. The cold was a welcome change, and we delighted in our snow dances and snowball battles. Rebecca demonstrated her skill at making a snow angel, and chortles echoed as we each carved our own images into a snowbank.

"Oh, it's beautiful out here," said Andrew.

"It looks like Mother's sugar frosting," said Rebecca.

"I've got an idea," said Andrew, rolling a large ball of snow before us. "Timothy Wells told me that in America they roll giant snowballs and then stack them, making it into a snowman."

"How fun," Millicent said excitedly. "Let's make one."

Jeremiah helped me push the growing ball of snow around the yard. It wasn't long before we had the body's snowballs ready to assemble. It took all five of us to lift them atop the huge one Andrew had first rolled.

Finally, after several attempts, the third ball was pushed atop the others and we had ourselves—

"Our first snowman!" proclaimed Rebecca.

"Let's give him a name," I prompted.

"But he hasn't a face yet," said Jeremiah.

"All right then, let's find some rocks and sticks, and we'll make him come alive." I cheered.

"We'll make it a happy face to welcome in our new baby," said Millicent proudly.

"Hurry, Jeremiah, let's get two branches for his arms," said Andrew. He grabbed his little brother's hand, and they were off. Then, remembering something, Andrew yelled back to us, "Timothy says they use a carrot for the nose."

"A carrot. How clever," said Millicent.

"Do we have a carrot in the root cellar?"

So Rebecca, Millicent, and I went scavenging to find some rocks for the snowman's face. Shortly we had a smile and eyes. Then, taking leave of the small group, I hollered, "I'll get a hat and a carrot for our man of snow. Think of a good name, and I'll be right back!"

Opening the door, I felt the warmth of the fire. It felt so good. Tiptoeing to the bedroom door, I listened. I could hear Mrs. Bottoms speaking with intense instructions. "Breathe deep, dear, and push hard again! Take another deep breath. Come on—push harder! I know you're tired, but I have got to get this baby boy to turn!"

"Boy?" I asked, opening the door to peek. "It's a boy?"

"Not yet, girl. We've got to get him here. I've got to get him to turn," Mrs. Bottoms said with a tone of frustration. "He's got his bottom where his head should be."

"Can I help?"

"Yes, girl." Walking me into the center of the kitchen, away from Miriam, she offered, "Mrs. Clark has got a breech baby, and try as I might—it isn't moving to help me any. Breech babies are always trouble. She is exhausted and flushed with the whole of it. I don't want to cut her open. There is the risk that, as tired as she is, I could lose them both." Immediately the fear of death shot through my mind.

"I hope that God has been listening to your prayers. We need His help now!" said Mrs. Bottoms with a firm conviction as we walked back to the bedroom. "Now!"

I wiped Miriam's face again. She looked so exhausted. It was seeing her in such pain that caused me to kneel once again by her side and hold her hand. It was then I heard a small voice whisper to my heart, "Push against her side with all your might." It chilled me to my inner soul, and I instantly started pushing.

"What do you think you are doing, child?" Mrs. Bottoms chastened me. "What on earth are you trying to do?"

I continued pushing, not paying one lick of attention to Mrs. Bottoms. Miriam just looked into my eyes with both wonder and intense pain. "Please, God, make this work!" I cried.

Then I witnessed with my own eyes a miracle. I saw Miriam's belly twist and turn, and suddenly Mrs. Bottoms yelled, "Well, I'll be! You've turned him! In all my years, I've never witnessed such a thing." Amazed, she wiped her face and continued almost gleeful, "Yes indeed, his head is ready in position. Dark black curly hair, I'll be! It's a miracle!" I stood in wonder as Mrs. Bottoms ordered, "One more big push, Miriam, and he's coming. Miriam, breathe and hold!"

It was the most exciting moment of my life when that tiny fellow let out his little whimper. Truly he must have been as tired as his mother. Miriam smiled at me, and I felt as if heaven had kissed my heart. With the good news, I rushed back outside and yelled, "He's here! Come see! You have a baby brother!"

Dropping their snowballs, rocks, and branches, everyone instantly ran for the house.

"But what about Mr. Snowman?" questioned Jeremiah.

"He'll wait. Our brother is here," said Rebecca, waving for him to follow.

Within a moment, all of us were surrounding the bedroom door. "Let's be real quiet, and we can hear him," I said.

Then, much like the parting of heaven's clouds, came another little cry. Instantly everyone leaped and danced about the room. Almost in united chorus we cheered, "He's here! He's here! He's finally here!" I sighed with delight and relief.

Immediately aware of all the excitement and noise, Mrs. Bottoms opened the door just wide enough for her strawberry red face to peek through. With a large smile, she removed the wet scarf from her head, "Praise the Lord—you have a baby brother."

My eyes filled with tears of gratitude for the gift of inspiration and for the love of a God who listens. I had felt that sweet feeling once before. I was so full of overwhelming joy, I stepped outside and looked into the heavens as the snow fluttered before my face. I said my own personal prayer of "thank you, thank you, thank you" and blew a kiss into heaven.

Spinning Delight

Early one morning when I was stirring the mush for breakfast, we heard sounds of horses and a sled outside the house. Even before we could pull back the curtains, we heard a loud voice.

"Ho, Ho, Ho! Merry Christmas!"

"It's Mr. Derrick! His wagon is filled with parcels and crates," said Miriam, opening the door.

"Wonder what he has for us," said Rebecca, peering through the window.

"Andrew, go see if you might be of service to Mr. Derrick," said Miriam.

Quickly donning his hat and coat, he rushed to be of help.

"Thank you, young man. I have a rather large crate to lift down from the wagon. Your assistance is greatly appreciated."

Reading the label on the front, Andrew announced, "It's from Ms. Eveline Gilbert, 45 Beckman Street, Broomhope, England. Who's that, Mother?"

"It's your grandfather's sister Eveline," said Miriam.

"Maybe it's something for Christmas," said Rebecca. We followed quickly behind Mr. Derrick and Andrew as they carried the large wooden crate to the center of the room.

"What is it, Mother?"

"I have no idea. I didn't know it was coming."

"Is it our Christmas?" asked Millicent.

"It took two of us to carry it. Must be something special," declared Andrew. "I'll get a wedge bar, and I'll have it opened in no time."

As Andrew went to the barn, we all gathered round with eager interest to see what the crate held. Between the antsy viewers, the creaking sounds of the wood breaking, and the nails stretching, our excitement grew. It took a few tries and then the lid came off.

"Straw?" Rebecca asked with a touch of disappointment. "Who wants straw?"

"I guess they put straw in to make sure it doesn't get bumped around and broken," said Andrew.

"I don't want a mess in here, so let me get a linen sheet on the floor first," said Miriam. "Place the straw on this sheet, please. This room isn't meant to be a barn."

"Let's dig in," I urged.

Like dogs looking for a bone, we dug into the crate and pulled out handful after handful of straw until Aunt Eveline's surprise was uncovered.

"What is it? Andrew asked.

"Looks like a bunch of wood pegs to me," Rebecca said, confused.

"I know what it is!" I squealed with delight, so loud that our new little baby was set to crying. "I'm sorry to have awakened Stephen, but this is a great day. Do you know what this is?" I grinned. Everyone looked stumped.

"It's a spinning wheel! I can hardly wait. I'll put it together."

Watching with piqued curiosity, the children marveled as I started pulling the pieces out and carefully placing them on the table. "It will take a little time, I know, but by night, we shall have a spinning wheel. Indeed, this is a great surprise as well as a blessing, you will see. We can make all kinds of beautiful yarns and threads, and then we can knit and crochet them."

One by one, I described the various wood pieces. "These are called the maidens. They are like thin fingers, and they hold the bobbin in place. This is the treadle, and it turns the wheel. This cord attaches to the pulley. See this marking, this WK? It's a Wilder Keene spinner. It's just like the one back home in our kitchen, except it's a little darker brown than Mother's." Jeremiah held one of the spindles in his hand. It was shaped like an hourglass. "It's a beautiful spinner," I explained.

Miriam looked a little overwhelmed, "I don't know how to spin."

"I'll teach you. I'll teach you all how to spin." I felt full happiness inside. It was like finding an old friend. "I can hardly wait for you to see it working."

When at last it was all pieced together, I gathered everyone around to see it. "It's ready, and it's a beautiful maple with leather joints." Sitting on the chair, I gave the first lesson on how to pump the treadle.

Pantomiming, as if I were holding yarn in hand, I described, "You take the thread from the sheep's fleece and feed it to the bobbins. You twist it carefully, spinning magic. You are going to love having a spinning wheel. I can hardly wait."

"Make the wheel go round, Hillary," begged Jeremiah.

Rocking my foot up and down upon the pedal gave instant rhythm and remembering. "Let me teach you a spinning song." The clacking sound of the treadle and flywheel gave accompaniment as the wheel spun around and around. "This is a song my mother taught me years and years ago. She told me that her great-grandmother taught her to sing it as well. I guess it's been in the family for nearly a hundred years." I sang aloud while I pumped the treadle and pretended to twist the yarn.

> *In the morning when the thread*
> *of sunlight breaks the dark*
> *I can see the glory of the Lord.*
>
> *As the clouds drift through the sky,*
> *in endless rippled joy*
> *I can see the glory of the Lord.*
>
> *There is light within the threads,*
> *To stitch a soul with love.*
> *Come gather round, and everyone come see*
> *'Tis a gift to be spinning, every day of your life*
> *A blessing for you and for me.*

The arrival of the spinning wheel was as good as Christmas morning to me. Spinning would take me on memory walks of times past. Hearing the clacking of the wheel gave me a sweet sense of home. I could close my eyes, and the sounds would call me back to when I was much younger. I could clearly see myself sitting on my mother's lap as she taught me. I could feel the fibers tickle my fingertips as we twisted the yarn. It was then that I learned to boil flowers and plants and make a variety of colors to dye the yarn.

I think that Miriam understood my attachment to the spinning wheel because she often encouraged me. "Hillary— might you spin awhile tonight? It gets baby Stephen to sleep faster." Believing I was helping both of us, I treasured the moments I had when spinning. I even taught the girls how to make dye. With help from the root cellar, we could use carrots and onions. When boiled together, they would make a brilliant orange. Miriam had stored some dried fennel, dandelion roots, and walnuts, which made a lovely shade of rusty brown. Jeremiah thought it was magic to see the yarn turn different colors.

Christmas Anticipation

"Smell how wonderful! Andrew cut some boughs for the mantle and hearth," announced Millicent as we carried armsful of freshly cut pines into the house.

"Lucky for us, we beat the storm. The dark clouds are gathering," I announced.

"It smells like the forest," said Miriam, moving the dishes off the dining table. "Put the pines here so we can clear the mantle."

"I love Christmas and all the festivities," I said with anticipation. "We always made pine wreaths and placed them on the windows and mantle. We would often string pinecones, popcorn, or berries. Sometimes we even used horse chestnuts. We made them into garlands," I said, indicating with artistic waves of my hands. "My mother would say,

'Now we'll add the finishing touch,' and she would dust the pine branches with sugar, making it look like freshly fallen snow. In just the right light, it would glisten. I loved it."

"Oh, I can hardly wait for Christmas," joined Rebecca. Then, becoming thoughtful, she asked gently, "What is your family going to do without you this Christmas?"

The simple question caused a flood of emotion to burst into my heart, but to distract Rebecca from noticing, I observed, "Look, it's raining outside now" and rushed to the window. The raindrops were forming little streams on the glass, mirroring the tears coursing down my cheeks. I pulled the curtains closed in an attempt to cover the intensity of my feelings. I gulped hard and said a simple prayer, "Help me, Lord, to hold my faith." Then, wiping my face, I said, "To answer your question, Rebecca, I'm not sure what they will do about Christmas. Mother is one to hold with traditions. She will probably make a fruitcake and place a surprise toy within it. I remember how fun it was to find it. Father will read from the Bible. He will insist on having a full English meal the Sunday before Christmas, and they will sing Christmas songs around our piano."

"Your family has a piano?" inquired Millicent.

"Do you play?" asked Andrew.

"Yes, all the girls in our house play the piano, even Anna. And before I left, Lucinda was learning how to play the violin as well. Listening to her play was a squeaky experience at first."

Andrew made sounds like a grating violin as he pretended to play. Everyone was amused by his actions and annoying sounds.

"My father would often say to us, as well as his congregation, 'Music is the key to salvation.'"

"Well then, we'd better start singing," Miriam said

decidedly. "Oh, come let us adore Him, Oh come let's drape the mantle, Oh come let's have some fun . . ."

I smiled and joined in singing, grateful that she had changed the topic. Music filled the room, and in spite of all the noise, baby Stephen fell asleep. Gently tucking him in the cradle, Miriam offered, "It will be a special Christmas, especially now, since we have him here. This is a time to rejoice, count our blessings, and thank the good Lord. What more could we want?"

"Chocolate balls!" answered Andrew.

"Chocolate balls?"

"Yes, and taffy and caramel corn."

"Vinegar taffy!"

"Vinegar taffy?" I yelped. "Eew! I've never had that, I don't think." I winced at the thought. "It doesn't even sound good—vinegar?"

"Oh, but it is!" said Andrew. "It's the best."

"You have got to try it," coaxed Millicent. "Our father always helps us make the taffy. Mother, might we make some today? It's raining, and our chores are all done."

"Please, Mother, it would be so fun with Hillary and everyone pulling."

I could see Miriam's mind thinking away. Then with a sudden smile and a nod of her head, she said, "Methinks it is a perfect day for a vinegar taffy pull. Now, everyone go wash your hands, and we'll get ready. Hillary and I will set about making it."

I pulled the large cooking pot from beneath the cupboard as Miriam flipped through her small wooden box filled with recipes. "I should have it memorized by now, but sometimes I forget how much sugar to add. Here it is—my trusty recipe for vinegar taffy. I can almost taste it now."

Placing the ingredients on the sideboard since the table

was filled with fir boughs, we began. "Hillary, I'll pour as you stir. Then it needs to boil till we get it into a hard ball stage."

"Smells awful!" I said, wrinkling my nose as I poured the vinegar from the bottle. "Four teaspoons isn't much, but it does make my eyes water."

"You're going to love it!" insisted Andrew when he returned to the kitchen. "We make it for Christmas—"

Suddenly, the front door opened, breaking into the chatter of the morning and startling everyone in the room. Standing tall in the frame of the door was a man, who bellowed, "Merry Christmas! And how might this good family be?" I stood in fixed fear, having never seen him before. Instinctively, I lifted up the stirring stick as if to beat him off. But before I could move, the children were running at him from every direction. Rebecca leaped into his arms, Andrew and Millicent clung tightly to his neck, and Jeremiah grabbed his legs.

"Papa, Papa!" Their voices rang with eager excitement. I realized then that this was their father. I stood silent and savored the scene, watching them kiss and hug. Miriam's face lit up with joy, and she rushed into his arms, saying, "Oh, this is the best day of all. You're home at last." I enviously watched as the continued squeals and dancing added to the spirit of Christmas in the room. I thought of my own anticipated reunion someday. In my heart's dream, there would be screams of delight, tears of joy, and endless hugs and kisses.

"Timothy, Timothy!" Miriam cried aloud as she rushed into his arms. "Christmas blessings," she said, hugging him tightly. "You are a heaven-sent miracle."

"And we have another miracle," said Andrew pointing to the wooden cradle.

"Yes, we have some very special people for you to meet," said Miriam, rushing to the wooden cradle and proudly lifting the tiny babe. "He came a bit earlier than expected. He's a miracle baby. We think he looks just like you, except for his dark hair. We named him Stephen Joseph Clark. He's a good baby and sleeps most of the time, thank the good Lord."

"Especially when Hillary works at the spinning wheel," added Millicent.

"Oh, and you need to meet our resident angel—this is Hillary Whitman. This is the young girl that you hired to help me with chores. Can I tell you how thankful I am that you insisted that we have additional help while you were gone? Life with Hillary in our home has been such a blessing. She's a lifesaver."

"She helped deliver Stephen Joseph," announced Andrew.

"She has taught us to spin and make soap. She does everything," Rebecca said proudly.

I stepped back as I felt my face blush at their compliments.

"Well, Miss Hillary, you sound like a hundred Christmas presents all wrapped into one gift. Sounds like you have been well worth every penny of our investment."

"Thank you. I love your family, Brother Clark," I said with a smile. "I think I have learned far more from them. I have learned how to milk a cow, make griddle cakes, and perform the duties of a mother, and I was just moments away from learning how to make vinegar taffy," I said squeamishly. "I don't like the smell of it, though."

"Vinegar taffy!" He cheered. "I'm just in time. Let's get stirring—can't have Christmas without taffy. It's a Clark family Christmas tradition, you know, and I wasn't about to miss it!"

CHAPTER IV

A Perfect Fit

IVING with the Clark family had been my delight and blessing for a little over three years. I relished the love that we shared. At three years of age, little Stephen loved sitting upon my lap as I worked at the spinning wheel, pumping and singing. It always seemed to me that he and I had a special connection. Perhaps it was because of the revelation I received and because I was the one who pushed him into the world. I don't know, but we did share a strong bond. He often delighted in the movement of the spinning wheel and watched the fine strand of thread twist as I gently held his small fingers upon the yarn, as my mother had done with me. I loved it when he would rock back and forth upon my lap as I sang.

> *In the morning when the thread*
> *of sunlight breaks the dark*
> *I can see the glory of the Lord.*
> *As the clouds drift through the sky,*
> *in endless rippled joy*
> *I can see the glory of the Lord.*

One day Miriam stood across the room crimping the crust on a pie shell, "You and Steven make a perfect picture sitting there together at the wheel, Hillary—sweet little boy and lilting music to melt the morning. We all love it when you sing that song. There is something that almost makes it sound like a prayer."

"My mother used to say that the words were healing to her, and I believe they have healed me as well," I shared.

"Hillary, do you remember the day that spinning wheel arrived? You were thrilled far more than any of us, and before the end of the day, you had it all put together. We were all so excited as we gathered round and you made the wheel spin."

"Everyone wanted a turn," I recalled.

"And then you taught us that song. It is a sweet melody. I think your mother must sing it often, just to recall your time together. Being a mother, I can only imagine, there is little question—she misses you so very much."

"Oh, I hope you are right. Spinning does take me home at times, and singing takes me to heaven in my thoughts," I revealed.

"Hillary, that is beautiful. Almost like scripture. 'Spinning takes me home, and singing takes me to heaven.' I love it." Then, after pondering a moment, she added, "Hillary, does missing your family get any easier with time?"

"Easier?" I paused. "I dream frequently of what it might be like going home someday. I dream that it will be a marvelous reunion and everyone is thrilled to have me back. Then there are those dark and scary nightmares. I find that my father still harbors resentment and bitterness. He slams the door in my face."

"Hillary, I can't imagine anyone harboring ill feelings against you."

"Well, for a while there, I was uncertain if I could close the door to my hurt. Then I opened my Christmas present from you—my little porcelain sewing thimble."

"It was just a simple thimble, Hillary."

"No, it wasn't just a simple thimble. I memorized the thought you attached to it: 'God can mend every broken heart, stitch any fault, and create with all power, that which has infinite possibilities.'

"I believe you knew that as I sewed with it on my finger, stitch by stitch, that thought would play over and over in my mind. It wasn't long before I was able to unpick the negative feelings and the hurt that I felt. It was a thimble full of wisdom that constantly reminded me of the need for forgiveness. Each night I pray that someday, somehow my family will be together again."

Burning Truth

A gust of wind rushed into the kitchen as Brother Clark opened the door. Yellow squash and orange pumpkins filled a large basket. "Can you close the door for me?" he yelled. "This is the last of the squash from the field. When the frost comes on the pumpkins, winter is knocking at the door." Bending over, he quickly gave Miriam a kiss on the cheek and said, "I see that pie crust is just waiting for the pumpkin filling. Pumpkin pie tonight!"

"Sounds good to me—warm pumpkin pie," I said, closing the door, "It's really getting colder out there."

"Oh, Hillary, by the way, I met Brother James in his buggy going past our field. I asked if he had heard anything of your family, as he had gone on business to Stafford."

Immediately my ears piqued with interest.

"To my surprise, he had. In fact, Brother James shared that he had met with some of the members of the Church on Sunday and had inquired about your father. It seems that of late your father has given real fire and brimstone sermons. They reported that he recently burned a copy of the Book of Mormon."

"Oh no, Father!" I cried in disbelief.

"Well, I guess if a large part of your congregation had left your—"

"It's all my fault, Brother Clark. My father wasn't at all like that when I was growing up. He was the closest example of an ideal man of God. He never would have done anything like that. Now, well, because of me . . ."

"Not because of you, Hillary, because of the truth of the gospel. He feels threatened, I'm sure."

"Oh, I can't believe it. Clearly, he must hate me." I buried my face in Stephen's little neck. My tears soaked into his shirt. Reacting to the news, I started to push quickly upon the treadle. My voice cracked as I tried to sing. I couldn't bear hearing about my father burning the Book of Mormon.

There is light within the threads,
to stitch a soul with love,
Come gather round, and everyone come see . . .

Placing his hand on my shoulder, Brother Clark said reassuringly, "Hillary, the past is past, and we cannot return to it. God would want for you to be valiant and strong and to follow Him. Things have a way of working out with the good Lord."

"I know that, Brother Clark. I am grateful that the Lord blessed the direction of my life that led me here to you and your family. I couldn't have been treated better. Certainly, I don't feel like hired help. I am forever grateful for that, especially since I realize you haven't had to keep me on this long either."

"What? And lose the best worker and teacher around?" Brother Clark said, smiling. "You are vital. Because of you, my daughters spin and knit, sing and dance, and Andrew learned to read. We've got jams and jellies that line the shelves, yarn, soap, and butter. Why, there aren't five people around who could replace you."

"You are indispensable." Miriam added with great vigor. "Hillary, never has there been a single thought to part with you or to send you on your way. Just like the yarn in that spinning wheel, you have spun yourself into our lives. You are more like a sister to me than a chore girl. Three years ago, I told Timothy that I had no need for hired help. Yet I am forever grateful that he insisted. When Elder Smithers walked you through that door, your eyes spoke volumes to my heart. I could almost feel your heart breaking. I knew you belonged right here. I know that God sent you to the Clark family. You have given all and more than I imagined possible. I am fortunate and blessed because of you, Hillary, and sometimes I feel guilty."

"Guilty?" I asked. Quickly placing Stephen on the floor, I moved to Miriam as she held out her arms toward me. I felt her tears run down her cheeks.

"Yes, I feel guilty. Guilty because your family must truly miss you, and we have you here with us. I have thought each year as we have sung Christmas carols, decorated the mantle, made candy, exchanged small gifts—even celebrated your birthday or canned strawberries—we have the blessing of you. Surely they must be thinking about you as well. It would be impossible, I believe, to cast someone out of the heart and mind. There must be an unending ache in their hearts."

"Oh, Miriam, you mustn't ever feel guilty. My father gave me a choice, and I believe I made a good one. Please realize that your family is a direct answer to prayer. These last years with you have strengthened my resolve and desire to be strong and faithful." Pausing for a moment and choking back the pain of memory, I shared, "When my father closed the door that dreadful day and said, 'Hillary Whitman is dead,' I felt my heart break. All the happiness in my life seemed to drain from me in an instant. To imagine my father deciding that my life was of little value to him if I believed differently was so hard. When I went to the elders and told them of my plight, they said to me that very day, 'Sister Whitman, the Lord looks after His sheep.' It was by the grace of God I was placed within your walls."

"Well, young lady," Brother Clark interjected. "With all this talk, I nearly forgot. While walking on Dormston Road, I happened upon Bishop Applegate speaking with Mrs. Bottoms. They were talking about the Book of Mormon."

"Really? And how is Mrs. Bottoms?" I asked. "Has the good bishop finally been able to convince her of the truth?"

"She's been a 'dyed-in-the-wool' Methodist for as long as I have known her."

"She would love my father then." I giggled.

"I did hear her say, 'Well I know that God heard Hillary Whitman's prayer. He told her to push that baby in such a way that the baby flipped right before my eyes. It was a miracle.'

"I heartily agreed with her, and then I added, 'If God listened to Hillary's prayer, and she was only fifteen, then do you think he could possibly answer a fourteen-year-old boy when he prayed?' You should have seen the look on her face—almost as pink and flushed as I have ever seen it. Hillary, I think Mrs. Bottoms may not be as 'dyed-in-the-wool' as we think."

Little Stephen stood patiently waiting by the spinning wheel and said, "Bin it, Hilly. Bin it."

"I haven't forgotten you, Stephen," I said, pulling him up on my lap. "We've got work to do, and we'd best be getting back to spinning. I have a good five skeins to make. And a penny and pence saved will bring me closer to Zion."

"Hillary, that reminds me. I have something for you."

Walking to the sideboard, Miriam reached into a drawer for a small purse. "This is yours. I have been saving it for you by request. It's been a while. Remember when the Belmont family was sick with the fever, and you went for a week and fixed them food and did the necessary chores for them?"

"Yes."

"Well, Mrs. Belmont said you wouldn't take money for that service. You told her you were merely being a good Samaritan." Placing the purse in my hands, Miriam continued, "She asked me to tuck this away until the time was right so that you might add it to your savings for America." Opening the purse, Miriam poured the coins into my hands. Excitedly, I started to count the coins. Stephen took instant interest and started to make my counting difficult. Setting him on the floor, I rushed to the oak table and spread the money upon it. "Bishop Applegate said I only needed a few more shillings. I can't believe it. I have enough! Enough money to make the purchase of my ticket to America. It's a miracle!" I threw my arms around Miriam, and together we danced around the room. I squealed, "I'm on my way to America!"

"You've worked so hard, Hillary, to earn every penny of it," said Miriam. "I'm so proud of you." Then, as tears welled in her eyes, Miriam became pensive. "You won't forget us, will you, Hillary?"

"Forget you?" I sighed, and my tears began falling faster than I could contain. "Never, no never."

Bound for America

"It seems that we might be in need of another bench or two," said Bishop Applegate, overlooking the congregation.

"And another box stove," whispered Brother Clark. "It's freezing cold in here."

In the back of the room, Brother Riggins was adding more wood to the stove. "I hope you feel the heat soon, or we all could look like frosted pumpkins shortly."

We all grinned and snuggled closer beneath a quilt. Tucking it between Millicent and Rebecca, I said, "We'll bring a few more blankets next week."

"I can still see my breath," said Andrew, "and we're inside."

Bishop Applegate, overhearing Andrew's comment, suggested, "Brother Andrew, might we call upon your able body to aid the making of music today? Thomas Gray is ill, and we need someone to pump the bellows for us. I guarantee that will warm you up quickly."

Tucking a scarf around his neck, Bishop Applegate welcomed, "Clearly, brothers and sisters, it is a cold morning. Yet I can feel of your warm hearts. We have much to be grateful for. By our numbers, we can see the gospel is reaching more families. In good time, we will be needing a larger space for our worship service. Remember," he said, looking around the room, "this once was a warehouse for gathering grains, and now we're gathering the Saints of the Lord. It is a joy to be together and join in song." He then nodded to Sister Copper at the organ, who in turn nodded at Andrew to start pumping the bellows.

Music soon filled the room. I have always been grateful that music has been a part of my life. I was taken home in thought. Even without closing my eyes, I could well imagine Father's church filled with people. I rejoiced in the melodies that lifted my praise unto God. To my surprise, my favorite melody was now being played on the organ by Sister Copper. I sat tall, opened the hymnal, and then sang with full voice.

All creatures of our God and King,
lift up your voice and with us sing.

I closed my eyes and said a little prayer. "Dear Father in Heaven, never let my family forget me, and someday help my father to forgive me." My thoughts were interrupted when I heard Bishop Applegate share some concluding thoughts.

"Can you believe it? In just a few weeks, we will be singing Christmas hymns. Oh, what a joyous time of year, to celebrate the life of our Savior, Jesus Christ. This holiday season, we will have great celebrations. We will have a live manger scene, a children's choir on Christmas Eve, and a Christmas social with all the decorations. But I have one Christmas wish of my own," he said, "Before you leave today, I must make mention of a matter I desire all of us to participate in. It's personal, but I feel it could be the perfect gift for one of our members. It has been four years since Hillary Whitman came to our little town of Sedgley. We all have been rewarded greatly with her presence. I know most of you feel as though she is an adopted daughter."

I felt my face turn red. I scanned the faces of Miriam and Timothy to see if they knew what was happening. They too seemed to be unaware.

He continued, "Most of us have been the beneficiaries of Miss Hillary's services and of her love." Looking at me, his voice broke with soft emotion, "It's hard to imagine her leaving us. Even though she was but a young girl when she arrived, she has enriched our lives, added sunshine to our days, and given us greater courage to stand for truth. She has been an example of one steadfast in her beliefs, faith, and desires. I know many of you have received Hillary's help in your homes. Some of you have purchased her heavenly scented bars of lavender soap, skeins of yarn, even some of her handiwork."

I felt as if the entire congregation's eyes were upon me.

"You know that it has been Hillary's goal and determination to join with the Saints in Zion. She has been diligent in her efforts to earn all monies to pay for her passage.

"Not long ago, I was speaking with Sister Clark, and I

asked her what would be one of Hillary's Christmas wishes. Instantly Sister Clark replied, 'Oh, I believe Hillary would love to see her family once more.' It was then that Sister Clark indicated that Hillary has earned enough money to purchase her ticket for passage to America."

A sense of pride in accomplishing my goal filled my soul with joy. My smile grew as I looked up at Bishop Applegate. Miriam squeezed my hand and smiled as well.

"Now, brothers and sisters, I believe it would be a great blessing for all of us to make an added wish for Hillary to come true. So today, upon your parting, if possible, might you place a small offering in the jar on the table by the door. I believe if we all joined together and donated a small amount, we will make it possible for her to travel to see her family in Stafford before leaving for America."

My heart beat faster, almost as fast as the tears filled my eyes. I nodded and smiled to express my appreciation.

After the closing prayer was offered, I was instantly surrounded by friends and well-wishers peppering me with questions.

"When will you leave?"

"How can I help?"

"How long since you have seen your family?"

"Do you know how much you shall be missed?"

"Do you have enough money to . . ."

Sister Applegate stood by the doorway, holding the jar now filled with money. Upon arriving at home, Brother Clark and I counted out the donated money. The members had been most generous.

"Young lady," he said, "I believe there is enough money here for you to travel to see your family." I gasped with surprise and joy.

"And," he started, "I have some other news as well that

might be of interest to you. I happened to be visiting with Sister Withers and learned that Brother Withers's sister just passed away. His sister lived in Hixon. Isn't that close to where your family lives?"

"Yes! Oh, yes," I bubbled. "Hixon is right next to Stafford.

Miriam interrupted, "You could write a letter and tell your family you're coming. Perhaps he could deliver a letter to your mother."

Hope filled my heart. "I must write a letter quickly and take it to Brother Withers. I must let them know of my leaving England. I pray I will see them again."

There was no time for perfect penmanship, so I hurried and wrote. If Brother Withers was to attend the funeral, he would surely be leaving shortly.

Dearest Mother,

I pray all is well with my family. My love for you remains strong, as well as my hope that your heartstrings have not been forever severed from me. My pillow is frequented with tears. Not one day has passed without thoughts of you all. Your absence has been a test for me.

I have lived and worked for a wonderful family named the Clarks. They have been a great blessing to me. I have grown in these years apart from you.

Before I forget, I must first thank you, Mother, for the skills I learned by your side. I have been able to help many here in Sedgley. It has also provided me a way to earn extra money. I have saved my money, and now I'm getting ready to make my way to America.

Before departing, however, I request but a moment's visit with you. I don't believe I can make my memories last much longer. I can't imagine another dream without a more recent picture of you and my sisters. If possible I would welcome a brief visit—as my Christmas wish.

I will be leaving Christmas Eve from Liverpool on the ship Marianna.

If all goes as I am planning, I will secure travel to Stafford, arriving there on Saturday, December the 17th in midday. Our good bishop, Brother Applegate, is arranging carriage transportation for me.

Hopefully, Father is keeping with his usual schedule, and will be away in preparation for his Sunday sermon. I pray the timing of my visit will be to your satisfaction. If you are desirous in seeing me once again, please tie a ribbon on the gate. That will be a signal that I can come home.

I don't believe the pain of parting ever goes away, at least not for me. Never has a day gone by without thoughts of you. It is difficult to imagine that you cannot mention my name, as every day I find myself sharing stories of my family. I believe the Clark family feels a kinship to you all because of it.

Words cannot express the need and desire of my heart to see you all again. After our visit, I shall journey to Liverpool, where I shall await my departure to America on Christmas Eve. I wish Father could understand me. I believe it is Father who set me on my course for Christ. I am grateful that, for the most part, my life was blessed with a compassionate, generous, and loving father.

I am learning that forgiveness is a gift from God, and I must open it each and every day.

Until we meet again, I shall be counting the days.

Forever Yours,

Hillary Whitman

Sealing the letter with a kiss, I tucked it into my coat pocket and set forth to the Withers's home. It was dark by the time I knocked on the door.

"Come in, come in, Hillary," greeted Sister Withers.

"What brings you out on such a cold winter's evening?"

asked Brother Withers, stepping to the front door and taking my hat.

"I heard your sister passed away recently. I am so sorry for your loss." He nodded with appreciation as I inquired, "Brother Clark thought you might be attending the funeral?"

"I am. I'm leaving in the morning at first light."

Searching his face, I asked, "I am hoping that you might carry this letter to my mother. She lives in Stafford, which is a neighboring town of Hixon. I need to get word to her. I wrote this letter hoping that they will see me before my parting."

"I understand," he said, looking directly at me, "By the sound of the tinkling jar today, I believe you will see your family, and I can only imagine the joy your visit will bring. I will personally give it to her. I can only imagine her delight."

"If at all possible, might you give it to her secretly? My father has destroyed my letters."

"I believe she will receive and welcome it."

"I hope you are right, Brother Withers."

Then I described, "Our house is a two-story, gray home situated south on Standon Road. There is a sign in the yard: 'Rev. William Whitman.' A large birch tree stands across the street from our house, which is surrounded with a white picket fence. You can't miss it."

Forever Linked

"I think the good Lord must have played a part in this reunion, Hillary," said Brother Smithers. "It seems like yesterday we stood on this very porch on another brisk morning. I remember you were a bit nervous then. Now, four years have passed, and we are blessed to travel together once more." Sliding my small suitcase on the floorboard of the buggy, he added, "Sorry, Miss Hillary, but you must say your good-byes quickly or you will miss catching the Midland at two."

In spite of the chilly morning, all of the Clark family stood on the porch perched like little birds sitting on a tree branch. Their faces had become so sweet to me. Since my coming, they all had grown so much taller and had grown so much within my heart.

I raised my voice, "Everyone, there is no way in the wide world that I can express my gratitude. Each one of you is a blessing in my life. I will never forget you."

"Here, Hillary, I want you to have this," said Millicent, placing a hand-knit blanket around my shoulders. I recognized it immediately and countered, "but that's the very first one you knitted."

"I know. I want you to remember that you taught me how to make it. There are a few mistakes in it, but no matter; it will keep you warm. It is my gift to you for Christmas." Stepping onto the buggy, Sister Clark tucked another quilt around my lap. I could see she was fighting the urge to cry, "Here, Hillary, you are bound to get cold. I don't believe one blanket is enough to keep you warm."

Andrew quickly carried out hot bricks from the fireplace. "Father says that if you place these bricks beneath your feet, they will keep your feet warm."

I looked into his blue eyes and saw the beginnings of a young man. "Now, don't go and get married just because your true love has left," I said with a grin. He blushed and escaped to the stairs.

I hugged Miriam tightly and whispered in her ear, "Thank you for always being there for me. I placed a canister of chocolate balls in the cupboard on the very top shelf behind the stirring pot. Give them to the children on Christmas morning. I know how they love them. It would give my heart delight to know that they might think of me for a moment that day. It will make my parting easier knowing each has a small remembrance."

Tears were clearly visible on everyone's cheeks as the moment of my departure arrived. "Now, every one of you will take a chill if you don't get inside," I cautioned, as my teeth were chattering louder.

Miriam held Stephen up, "Say good-bye to Hillary." Then without controlling her tears, Miriam released the deep emotion held within her heart and said, "I love you, Hillary. Always, always, remember that you are cherished."

I released my emotions as well, raised my hand and hanky dramatically, and smiled. "I will write as soon as I arrive in America." Now looking directly at every face, I took a deep breath in an effort to hold back the tears. "I am forever linked to your hearts for all eternity. With God's help I will see you again."

"That will be a joyous day for all, Hillary," said Brother Clark, embracing Miriam tighter to surround her in arms of comfort.

Brother Smithers tipped his hat and clicked his tongue, "Giddy up, Mazie. We must be leaving before the tears turn into a river and we need a boat." With that, he squeezed my hand.

Blowing kisses, I added, "God be with you all, and may the heavenly angels watch over and protect you. Till we meet again!" Leaning against the seat, I watched as the little family, who for the last four years had been mine, disappeared from view.

CHAPTER V

Greater Courage

Stafford, England
December 17, 1839

USTERING my courage and holding my excitement, I stood beneath the large birch tree as I scanned the house.

"Yes!" A bright green ribbon was tied to the front gate. "Yes, yes, they want me!" I took a deep breath of determination, gathered my skirts, and before doubt could enter in, I ran for the front porch. Almost in announcement, the old gate squeaked as I pushed it open. My heart pounded heavy. I burst into the foyer and hollered, "I'm home!"

Almost shocked by my bold behavior, I stood frozen. Then a sudden squeal sounded as Lucinda came running toward me. The wooden floor intensified the sound of her steps.

"Hillary! She's here, everyone—Hillary's home!" Lucinda cried aloud, shattering the quiet. Instantly tears turned into sobs and tight embraces.

"Hillary! Hillary!" called my mother, rushing to my side. "Thank heavens! At last, you are here!"

I was thrilled as I saw Anna come running. "Hillary, you didn't forget me, did you?" she asked, jumping with delight to be included in the dancing circle. It was just like I had envisioned it would be. I felt as if I were in heaven. My heart leaped with joy. My tears . . . well, I didn't want to stop them from falling because they seemed to wash away all the hurt.

"Oh no, I never forgot you for even a moment, Anna. I can't believe it. Look at you all." Running my fingertips through Anna's auburn curls, I said, "You're nearly as tall as me." Then, looking at Lucinda and quickly surveying her changes, I said, "You're even more beautiful than I remember."

Mother stood momentarily immovable, with tears rolling down her cheeks. Finally gaining a touch of composure, she spoke. "It's so good to see you, Hillary. You're the one who has grown up. I see it in your face."

Once again, Mother embraced me, and I held her tight and said, "I don't ever want to let you go."

Then with a deliberate tone, Mother said, "Hillary, please don't ever think we washed you from our thoughts. Your name has never left our lips."

Lucinda exclaimed, "This has been the longest day of my life! We've been up since before dawn, and the hours have dragged by waiting for you."

Then to my surprise, Mother yelled as loud as I have ever heard her, as if to proclaim it from the rooftop, "Hillary, Hillary, Hillary Whitman is alive and well!" I was shocked by her action, and Lucinda and Anna reflected their amazement as well. "Everyday your sisters and I knelt together in prayer and asked God to bless and protect you."

Looking directly at the three faces streaked with tears, I paused to capture the moment. "It's just like I imagined: tears, screams, hugs, and dancing circles. This is what family is for." Breathing deep, I gathered my words. "My prayer is that this feeling held within my heart—this very moment—is eternal. I have often dreamed and envisioned you all. I have painted pictures in my mind, so afraid that with time I might forget. How often I would try to visualize you, Mother, sitting at the spinning wheel or Anna stitching on a sampler. Believe me when I say, I have even missed hearing you play your violin, Lucinda," I said in jest.

"She's getting better at it, Hillary," said Anna.

"I missed the sound of your voice, Mother. I longed for the scent of your perfume and for your embraces that always melted my fears. Words cannot begin . . ."

"Even though Father says we can't speak of you, we do," smiled Anna, "in secret."

I laughed aloud, "I have truly missed your contagious giggle, Anna, and how I have longed to talk with you, Lucinda. I have even missed the squabbles over dishes and our daily chores. But I'm here now, and even if it is a moment, I shall cherish every morsel of it. You can't imagine how wonderful it was for me to see my home again and then to see the ribbon on the gate."

"I tied it there," Anna said, grinning.

"I am just thankful you wanted to see me again!"

"See you again? Dear daughter, we have been so excited ever since I met your Brother Withers and read your letter. For the three of us, it's been like Christmas just knowing that you were coming."

"Fourteen days of waiting is impossible," said Anna.

"Keeping your visit a secret—well, I came close to letting it slip from my lips," said Lucinda.

"Me too!" said Anna.

Glancing at the mantle clock surrounded by a Christmas garland of pines, holly berries, and pinecones, I noted regretfully, "I shall miss another Christmas with you. But seeing you is the greatest gift I could ask for." Holding them one by one in my arms to secure a lasting impression, I added, "I love you *so* much! I prayed constantly that I would be able to see you. I have feared greatly that Father might thwart my plans."

"Mother made sure he was helping a neighbor. He'll be gone for a while," reassured Lucinda.

"Brother Bowman said that Father is still much opposed to the missionaries and that even in public he has taken to burning our scriptures."

"Father is most firm in everything. He's unrelenting, and if someone mentions those Mormons . . . well . . ."

"Deep down, Hillary, I know he thinks of you," Mother said. "One night I saw him stand outside your room, looking at your bed. I believe he has let pride and fear fill his heart."

"Hillary, did you know that Father hung a black wreath on the door when you left?" asked Anna. "It means that someone has died."

"Shhh! You shouldn't have told her that!" Lucinda said sternly.

"A black wreath?" I asked, thinking for a moment. Then, catching myself, I continued, "Well, I like the green bow on the gate better. This is the best of holidays! From the look of the evergreens and garlands, you've got everything ready for Christmas. However, I have no gifts to give you for Christmas. It took every shilling and penny I had to pay for my passage to America. I would ask a favor of you all."

"Yes, anything, Hillary," said Mother, looking intently in my face.

"Sister Clancey taught me how to make memory locks and forget-me-knots from strands of hair. I need but a small clipping from each of you. I will have plenty of time on the ship to weave your hair into flowers. Then I will place it in a locket. It will be a treasure for me to keep till we meet again."

My mother eagerly shared, "Yes, I had one once of my grandmother's. I'll get the scissors, and you can have a snippet from each of us. You'll have to cut the curls, Hillary.

I just want to look at you for as long as possible." Mother handed me the shears quickly and began to cry.

Taking a long strand of Anna's hair, I shared, "Rebecca, one of the girls I cared for, has hair almost the same color as yours. She probably thought it strange of me to want to comb it so often, yet, somehow, I felt as though I was brushing yours. It always brought back sweet memories of those nights when I would brush your hair till it glistened like a sunset on the lake. I'll just clip a little curl, Anna. It will grow back."

"And here is mine," said Lucinda. But even before I could clip it, she threw her arms around me tightly and wept openly. "Hillary, I don't want to lose you again."

"Lucinda . . . God willing, I will see you again. We will be together someday. You are woven into my heart, and we are sisters, eternally bound." Taking a snippet of her hair, I said, "There, I have a piece of you." Then I took a piece of my own hair and, clipping a curl, said, "Now you have a part of me to remember." I placed it in Lucinda's hand. "You must promise to keep me in your prayers."

"Hillary," Mother said, pausing in thought. "Oh, we . . ." she paused, as if something rested heavily on her mind. "Later."

Glancing at the clock, I nervously announced, "I know I must leave. I can't stay longer. I cannot miss my carriage. I must take a final look around and forever imprint it upon my mind." Then, gathering them all in one loving cluster, I squeezed them tight. "I wish my visit could be longer. Each moment has been delicious. This visit is an answer to my many prayers."

Drawing a letter from her apron pocket, Mother slipped it tenderly into my hands, "I have penned you a letter, dear one. Please hold it unopened until you are well upon the sea and not a moment before. Promise me?"

"I promise, Mother, and I will hold it close to my heart," I said, tucking it beneath my bodice. "I shall treasure each word and read it over and over again. Now, I must be going!" Instinctively, everyone embraced me tightly. Eyes welled with tears, and sobbing sounds mixed together with crescendos of "I love you, I love you."

"I almost forgot!" Anna squealed before running to the bureau drawer. "I made you something for Christmas. Hurry! Open it!" she insisted. I quickly unwrapped the muslin and untied the string, revealing a little angel made from a wooden peg. I smiled as I held her up. "Anna, she's darling. I love how you made her halo out of wire and her wings of lace. She will dance with me to America," I said, twirling my angel in the air.

"I made her small enough so you could hold her in your hand and feel of my love. When you hold her tightly and pray, she will carry your prayers to God."

"Oh, she's precious, Anna. I will call her my Angel Anna, after you, and kiss her every day." I drew Anna into a tender embrace.

Unwavering Faith

Suddenly the front door opened. Fear froze our small circle. My eyes widened and a jolt of fear rushed up my spine.

"Father!" Lucinda gasped.

"What is this gathering?" Reviewing the sight and the visitor, my father paused in suspended thought. Then, flaring with bitter intensity, he added, "A secret reunion of sorts, I guess. A prodigal daughter returns?"

"William!" protested my mother. "Not now, she's—"

"Thinking she might come home? Might you have changed your mind? Perchance you have grown somewhat wiser in four years? Are you still mesmerized by those Mormons? Maybe you have discovered Joe Smith's story to be a tall tale and your golden book to be a farce," he said smugly and laughed loudly.

I watched as my mother drew a breath and insisted, "Not now, William. She's leaving . . ."

Looking up into his face, I stepped closer, gathering strength and courage. I knew I must stand firm against the intense wind of his words. Firmly but softly, I spoke, "Father, I am leaving, but the desire of every inch of my heart is to be home with my family. I have only dreamed and prayed to be with you all, joined forever and eternally. Having a family and living in happiness are the object of this life."

Tears had no place now as I knew my degree of conviction and that I must stand impervious to his treatment. "Do you not see, Father? It is you who taught me to be true to my spirit. It is you who opened my heart to the light of my Savior. You instilled within me the desire to follow Christ. Sermon upon sermon, you asked everyone 'to pick up the cross' and follow Him. Because of my love for my Heavenly Father and Jesus Christ, I have come to believe the way I do. I . . . I must follow my belief and the love of our Master."

"Love of God, girl—I preach it!" he interrupted with surging anger on his face.

I continued, unwavering, "Father, if I cannot enjoy the eternal, everlasting truths and blessings of the gospel of Jesus Christ under this very roof—my home, with my family that I love—then I must go where I can. I know with full soul and testimony that I have found more truths within the scriptures. I have found answers to questions, and I have felt something strong within my heart where it burns. I cannot and will not deny what I have found. I have spent years in study—"

"Your golden Bible," he jested.

"I cannot deny or hide my feelings, Father." Breathing deeply, I softened my voice. "Father, being separated from those I love . . . has been truly a test of my heart and faith. Yet, if I must, I can stand alone."

"Stubborn, unrelenting child, have it your way! You are never to step within these walls again, or I will have you arrested." He spoke with a searing chill, then, looking squarely at Mother and the girls, he directed, "Evidently, some have gone against my will and openly welcomed this lost lamb. But I insist she will never be mentioned again. Abruptly pulling the door open, he motioned for me to depart.

"William!" exclaimed Mother.

Farewell, England

Liverpool, England
December 24, 1839

The sound of seagulls made me keenly aware that I must be nearing the Waterloo Dock. I had reached Liverpool at last. I was filled to overflowing with excitement as well as anxiety. I had checked and rechecked my suitcase and satchel, securing my ticket and identification.

"Are you sailing on the Marianna," asked a porter, pointing. "She's fit and ready to sail."

I had never seen a ship before. I marveled as it sat motionless and stately upon the dark green water, contrasted by the dock brimming with excitement. Noises of eagerly awaiting passengers filled the morning air. Already, at eight, it was a brisk gray day.

Four years of preparation and saving pound and penny

finally found me at my place of departure, Liverpool, England. Seamen were yelling forth orders. "Stand by your lines!" "Pipe down!" "Heave the log!" They made no sense to me and added to the overwhelming uncertainty of it all. Unknown faces filled the morning canvas as I listened to the variety of languages. Nervously I tapped my feet and clicked my shoes together. The line of embarking passengers seemed endless. Never had I seen so many people. It was a time of intense confusion and yet it was filled with hopes and dreams of brighter tomorrows. Donkey carts filled the dock, packed with worldly stores, the merchants seeking a pence or shilling before the final call, perchance to sell a Christmas trinket or some extra food. Piles of boxes, trunks, and bundles lined the dock. It was difficult to see across the platform, filling the moments with restless jitters.

Bishop Applegate had warned me of the possible thieves at the dock, saying, "There seems to be a secret league, a conspiracy, to fleece and pluck immigrants without mercy and pick their pockets on the dock. A ticket to America is truly a treasured item, and many might try steal it. Hold it close and protect it!" How well I knew the worth of my ticket. It had taken four years to finally provide sufficient funds for my passage.

I sat for a moment upon the huge rope securing the ship to the dock, taking a last look at my England. Fearful, I pulled my wool shawl tighter around my shoulders while I watched my puffs of breath drift into nothingness. I thought for a moment, would I become just like the puffs of white— would I become as nothing, forgotten to my family? With no pictures to recall, would my memories fade? Could I ever forget the last words I heard my father speak? I bit my lip so as to stop it from quivering as I recalled those haunting words, "Her name will never be mentioned again in this home!"

Then, like a sliver of hope confirming my decision, I recalled the words so often spoken in my father's sermons. I could almost hear him pound upon the pulpit and proclaim in the stirring words of the Master, "He that loveth father or mother more than me is not worthy of me: and he that loveth son or daughter more than me is not worthy of me. And he that taketh not his cross, and followeth after me, is not worthy of me."

"Oh, Father, I am not dead to God. I know God is well aware of me, and I will follow Him," I said softly with firm resolve. "I am worthy of His love, and I shan't think of that awful moment again, be it to preserve my life."

Distracted by a loud noise, I watched a young boy stand on the ship and sound his bugle. Then a seaman bellowed, "First call for the Marianna," drawing me to my feet. I clasped my small satchel even tighter, which contained my necessary papers and tickets and moved in the direction of the boarding plank.

The crowd drew together into massive lines of confusion. A woman with three small children huddled on the platform beside me inquired, "Are you alone, miss?" as her wide-eyed children focused on my face.

"I am never alone," I said with a sense of caution.

"Might you be able to hold my wee babe until we board? I haven't enough arms to carry him. Between the luggage, the children, and traveling alone without any husband . . ."

"Oh, I'm sorry. Yes, please let me take him. I'll be happy to assist you," I declared. Holding the child and looking into his large blue eyes, I asked, "What is your name, little fellow?"

"He's Albert. Albert Sullivan McGuire, and I am Benjamin McGuire. My baby brother is eight months old," said a boy looking about the age of Jeremiah Clark. I watched as the young mother began awkwardly gathering up an armful of luggage while reaching for the hand of her young daughter.

"We're going to Zion," proclaimed Benjamin, loaded with two large carpetbags.

"Zion! Me too! Might you be Latter-day Saints?" I eagerly inquired.

Almost as eagerly as I inquired, she answered, "Oh, yes, through and through. In fact, there are at least twenty-five of us boarding from Wigan, England."

"I am a Latter-day Saint as well." I smiled, feeling instant kinship.

Holding to the railing and trying to balance both child and luggage made me appreciate the mother's struggles. Looking at the dark water lapping against the ship made me afraid.

"Don't look down. Face forward and up," she said, sensing my fear. "Are you afraid of water?"

"I'm not sure of the sea. I've only swum in a pond before. But I do like your thought, 'face forward and up,'" I said. "And my name is Hillary Whitman."

"Pleased to make your acquaintance," she said, "and to receive your help. I'm Martha McGuire."

The boarding line inched closer to the deck. Luggage and children were scooted forward. No sooner had I reached the top of the loading platform than I was greeted by a demanding voice, "I need to see your boarding pass, miss." Trying to juggle child and luggage was difficult, and his impatience was marked by a stern stare. "Is this your child?"

"No, I am just holding him for that woman," I said, pointing. "As you can see, her arms are full."

"Stand here and don't move. We won't be having any stowaways on this ship!"

"Stowaway? He's with her, and I have my own ticket." I drew it out.

"Don't move. I'll check," he said curtly.

I watched as he questioned her and checked her tickets. I breathed better when he returned and announced, "Yes, she has duly paid for passage for the lad as well, but sometimes it is a trick to avoid payment. Now, might I have your pass, miss?" I handed it to him proudly.

"Hillary Whitman. Yes—you are noted."

Then another man following closely behind him stepped forward, "Open your mouth, miss." Looking at his badge, I saw he was the ship's surgeon. Standing directly in front of me, he said, "Open!" Then he stuck a stick within my mouth and looked intently into my throat. I stretched my tongue forth. "Ah."

"Been ill, sick, or with the fever within a week?" He spoke with routine rhythm.

"No!"

I watched as he initialed my boarding voucher. "Approved! Next!" he bellowed.

I followed the path and direction of the other passengers. Close behind the doctor, the ship's agent took my well-guarded passage ticket and stamped it. It was then that little Albert started to cry. Remembering my little angel in my jacket pocket, I drew it forth in hopes to entertain him. Angel Anna danced upon the morning air and drew smiles from little Albert.

"Miss, might I see your passage ticket?" asked another officer. Circling a number, he directed me toward the stairs. Steep stairs provided the only entrance to the steerage below the deck. My eyes had to adjust to the darkness. I followed the purser, distinguished by his brass buttons, cap, and blue wool coat. Breathing a little more securely, I said aloud, "We're on our way to America, Albert—one step closer to Zion."

Another young man dressed in the same blue uniform

with brass buttons looked at Sister McGuire and said, "Families stay in the ship's hold, and it is that way," he said, pointing. "And you, miss, are in the after-berth, in the opposite direction." Realizing that we must part, Sister McGuire reached out for little Albert. "We'll meet again soon, I'm sure. Thank you for your kindness in helping me. We will follow the purser and find our space."

Thank heavens I saw another man in the same outfit with brass buttons. "Might you show me to my space?" I asked "It's so dark down here. How does one see?"

"Miss, most of us get used to it. You will as well."

The only lights below came from a few lamps placed in strategic locations that shed a dim yellow glow. It was quickly apparent to me he had little need for light to see, as he was familiar with the surroundings. Soon I discovered that what I thought were chicken coops piled atop one another, were in fact berths made of rough lumber to sleep in. In the upper compartments it was barely possible to sit upright, while the lower spaces had a bit more room. Thank heavens Bishop Applegate insisted I have a lower berth.

"Here it is, miss. Berth number thirty-seven. Then he said routinely, "one mattress, one blanket, one bucket, one spoon, and one tin cup—as paid for. This is your new home," he said, nodding as he checked my name off the passenger log. Then he informed me, "Miss Whitman, listen for the roll call. You will need to make your way to the upper deck before we cast off."

"Thank you," I said as he walked away and I looked at my new "home." "And thank you, Lord," I added in gratitude as I realized that one of the few lanterns in the hold had been placed on a platform directly across from my bed. Darkness had always been a fear of mine, so even that small light was welcome.

I spread the heavy gray blanket out and placed my suitcase on the corner of my mattress tick, leaving just enough room to curl up on. Indeed it was a blessing to be of small stature in the limited space. Busy noises filled the darkness as people continued to push suitcases, bundles, and trunks into simple spaces. I felt sorry as I heard countless children crying. I sensed their fear of the unknown.

Realizing that my quarters were tight and there was only one of me, I wondered about the conditions of the McGuire family. Retracing my steps and moving cautiously between boxes and bustling people, I voiced aloud as I entered the crowded hold, "Sister McGuire? Sister McGuire?" Surely I must have appeared to be a stray child seeking a parent, as I heard, "Not here, not here, child." I was relieved when at last I heard a soft voice rise from the dim lights, "Over here. I'm over here." Crowded into a small berth was the family. "I'm trying to get Elise and Albert to sleep, but I'm afraid there is just too much noise," she said, draping a blanket over the berth to buffer some of the noise.

"I came to see if I might be of help. Perhaps if I take Albert to my space and cradle him there, he might sleep some. It's not as noisy there."

"Oh, I would so welcome it."

"Albert, would you like to play with my Angel Anna?" I asked, smiling. "Come with me." A smile grew on his face, and he reached out for my arms.

"I think our Albert is taken with you," said his mother.

"No, I just think he likes my angel. I'll try and get him to sleep, but if you should need me, I am in the after-berth in number thirty-seven. It's where all the single young girls stay."

"You are an angel, Hillary. Taking Albert would be such a blessing," she said, kissing him on the forehead.

Albert was still restless and crying a touch, so I rocked him on the corner of my bunk. "Let's see, my angel can dance for you again. My sister Anna made her for me. She is my Christmas present." Holding Albert upon my lap, I dangled Angel Anna. "I shall sing you a lullaby, and you can watch while Anna dances. Shh!" I said softly as I began the lullaby.

> *Father, watch thy tender sheep,*
> *Watch and care—while they sleep.*
> *Tender words all filled with love.*
> *Whispering angels—from above.*
> *Sleep, little child, let peace find place.*
> *Feel God's love upon your face.*

Albert's eyes closed, and I continued singing as I found my own comfort in the melody. In the dimness, my mind flooded with thoughts of home, my sisters, Mother, and those last moments with them. I then thought of the Clark family. Each one had a place within my heart. Facing toward the darkness and curling closer to Albert, I drew my blanket, the one Millicent had made, around my body. Tears filled my eyes, and I could feel them flow steadily down my cheeks. Taking a moment, I said a prayer, "Give me strength, dear Father, for I am leaving all that I love." It was upon wiping my face with my sleeve that I felt the letter rustle within my blouse. Remembering it, I eagerly sat up and pulled the letter out. Mother had said I was to wait until I was upon the sea, but that could be hours. I thought to myself that she would clearly understand my dire need and desire. So breaking the seal, I whispered aloud with regret, "I know I promised you, Mother, but I cannot wait until we take to sea." Placing my blanket over little Albert, I drew closer to the light from the lantern and began to read.

Broken Promise

Dearest Hillary,

My precious daughter, they say parting brings sorrow to the heart. I believe that to be true. With your absence of over four years now, I have been forced to seek the peace by which a mother's soul can survive. My ears have been continuously open for any word, knowledge, or news of you. I cannot conceive the thought that I am supposed to erase my feelings for my daughter Hillary. You are my bright-eyed, beautiful daughter. Regardless of the enforced rule of your father, your sisters and I have talked of you continually. We have even celebrated your birthdays in secret. We have prayed each night for you and your safety. I cannot begin to fathom an eternity without you, Hillary. A mother kissing her child for one last time? I cannot imagine it, and I believe God would not have it so.

A voice interrupted my reading, as well as my tears. "Miss, I'm Elder Christian Larson. I am taking the roll for the members of the Church of Jesus Christ of Latter-day Saints. Might you be one?" he asked.

"Oh, yes!" I smiled, "Bishop Applegate said there would be a leader on board, and right now, I feel the need for a kindred spirit."

"You do look like you are a touch unsettled," he replied. "Tell me your name."

"I'm Hillary Whitman, from Sedgley, England." I'm sure he could see my tear-streaked cheeks.

"I'm sorry to have interrupted you."

"I was reading a letter from my mother. Just the thought of leaving England and my family is so hard. I might never see them again."

"God willing, we all will be with loved ones someday. I am most happy to meet you, Miss Hillary. I have been asked to shepherd some 220 Saints aboard the Marianna." Looking over at Albert sleeping, "Oh, and I see you have a little one . . ."

"Oh, no. He's not mine. He belongs to the McGuires. They are members too. I'm just trying to settle him a bit. I have a little more room here in my berth."

"I will let you alone with your reading and check back with you later," he said, tipping his hat.

"That would be so appreciated. I feel much calmer just knowing you are on board."

I opened my letter again. I could see where my tears had left their mark. If not careful, I would surely smudge it and render it unreadable by my tears.

Despite your father closing one door, we have you to thank for opening another. Four years ago, the reality that our daughter had been torn from my arms and sent away brought much contention to our home. Our family was broken. Bitterness grew in my heart. My world as I knew it was instantly changed because of another religion. At first, I admit, I was angry with you. Then I was stirred with anger against your father that he would send you away. I fought fear, anger, and contempt and found little peace in any corner of my heart. I cried till I could cry no longer. I couldn't find any peace or hope. Finally, after days of arguments and endless discussions with your father, I chose to not sleep with him.

I longed for you, Hillary. It was then that I crawled upon your bed, with hopes that it might bring some form of comfort. It was while upon your pillow, crying for want of your face, that I felt something hard beneath the pillow. I found your 'treasured book' where, I believe, you knew I would find it. At first I threw it to the floor in despair and despised it, for it was but an evil wedge in our family. I threw it into the dresser drawer. I had no need for it. Yet, within days, something swelled in my soul and pushed me to return to the drawer. Now, mind you, I at first had no need for it, but I was directed in spirit to open it and to read it. I found a phrase that caught my soul unawares. You had underlined it: Ether 4:11. "He that believeth these things which I have spoken, him will I visit with the manifestations of my Spirit, and he shall know and bear record. For because of my Spirit he shall know that these things are true; for it persuadeth men to do good."

I immediately thought of you, Hillary, and those feelings that you held so firmly. Perhaps it was because of your unwavering belief. But by some miracle of God, the feelings I had toward the book—

"I'm sorry, miss, to disturb you again," said Elder Larson, "but did you say your name is Whitman?"

"Yes."

"Do you have other family traveling?"

"No, I'm traveling alone. My father is a Methodist minister and very much opposed to me joining the Church. I have no family with me."

"Well, perhaps they are distant relatives of yours. How do you spell your name?" he said, looking down at his roster.

I started to spell my name slowly. "W-h-i-t—"

"M-a-n!" came loudly from beyond the crates and barrels. Before I could continue, there was Lucinda, like magic, before my eyes. Then Anna dashed from the darkness and jumped beside me. Between the hugs and elated cries of delight it was a glorious, chaotic moment. Albert and Elder Larson were clearly caught by surprise as I jubilantly screamed, "What are you doing here? What is this? What in the world are you doing here? Does Mother know?"

Then in answer to my question, Mother popped her head around a large crate. Having no more arms to go around, I allowed Mother to hold my face in her hands. She spoke in a teasing tone, "Hillary Whitman, you forgot in all haste to get a clipping of my hair. How will you remember me?" She smiled with a twinkle and wink of her eye.

Albert began to cry louder. I picked him up and started to bounce him to soothe his fear.

"I can't believe this. What is happening? How . . ." I questioned.

Then, looking gently into my eyes with a somewhat serious look, my mother said, "I believe, Miss Hillary Whitman, you broke your promise. I saw you reading my letter before you were at sea."

"I know I did, but I couldn't wait. My heart was bursting with thoughts of leaving you all in England. I had to read it. I was feeling so forlorn . . ."

"It's all right, Hillary. We thought to surprise you. We were going to wait to surprise you until we had left the port."

"And were headed to America," said Anna excitedly.

Then, looking with a smile at Elder Larson, "Somehow our secret couldn't be had. Yet, it looks like in the all around, we did surprise her."

Picking up the letter from the floor, Mother handed it to me and said, "I was watching you and I believe you haven't finished reading it yet—read on!"

"I don't know if I can. I am so excited. But why are you here?"

"Read, Hillary," she insisted, motioning to the letter.

Lucinda took Albert from my arms, and I continued my reading, my heart beating intensely, as all eyes were upon me.

. . . and those feelings that you held so firmly . . .

Lucinda told me how she rescued your book from the compost so that you could study. Well, we too studied, your sisters and I—in secret. We would read it after chores were done and while your father was away. I, along with Lucinda and Anna, have read it cover to cover twice.

I looked into their faces with shock and amazement and exclaimed, "I can't believe it! You've all read the Book of Mormon?"

I could see my sisters bubbling with words they wanted to say, but Mother simply said, "You have to read the whole letter."

I sighed and quickly returned to the pages, although the words were blurred by my tears.

I must share a miracle with you. One night before we could hide our copy of the Book of Mormon, your father sat right down at the kitchen table where we had been reading. The Bible rested next to it. You can only imagine our intense fear when he even touched the book, but he clearly didn't see it. Since your father has taken to burning the Book of Mormon, we feel that it was a blessing directly from God, protecting our copy.

There was a feeling of guilt as we watched your father grow in his bitterness toward the Saints. I at one point asked him, "What if it is true, William—this gospel that so many of your congregation have chosen to believe?" Words cannot express his anger or his threatening words as I voiced my questions. He told me that he would take Lucinda and Anna from me if I crossed him in any way. Your father's spirit has become heavy and dark. Bitterness and darkness have grown within him. It seems he trusts no one. Somehow, I believe, he is haunted by your unrelenting belief.

After reading the Book of Mormon, we have been blessed with a testimony of the profound truth and cannot deny it! I know now what you meant when you said you had a 'burning in your soul.' I too have felt that burning inside, and so we secretly sought the missionaries. Realizing that at some point we must tell him, I knew that we must be prepared to lose all. So your sisters and I have kept busy with the loom, crocheting collars, and making skeins of thread to barter. In secret we have tucked away money. It was with the hope we would be able to find you. Then when Brother Withers came with your letter telling us when and where you were going, it came as an answer to prayer. We knew God was well aware of us. In brief, Lucinda, Anna, and I are waiting to join ourselves in baptism. We are desirous to become members of the Church of Jesus Christ of Latter-day Saints.

Stunned with joy, I exclaimed, "Baptized! I can't believe it! Oh, Mother." Pulling her close, I sobbed uncontrollably. After a few moments, Lucinda spoke, "I'll finish the letter, Hillary."

If our plans are successful, we will be found aboard the Marianna, and we will sail with you. We will celebrate Christmas together. Till then, my precious Hillary, know how much we love you.

With tenderness,
Mother

CHAPTER VI

Oh, Say but I'm Glad

OLDING my face gently and wiping my endless tears, Mother continued, "I took great courage from you, Hillary Whitman, as well as from God. When William said that by law he could take my girls and render me without home or family, I was pressed to make a choice. I vowed I would not lose another daughter. Your father is stubborn, at best, determined in his stand. We have kept all this a secret from him, even our parting.

The missionaries were most helpful in securing our tickets and travel plans in secret. We were most thankful for your letter, for you had indicated the date of your departure on the Marianna. In secret we packed our belongings and slipped away without your father's knowledge. It took every inch of courage to press onward. I can well understand and imagine how you must have felt leaving us, Hillary. It has been four long years without you."

The ship's bells rang and everyone was ordered to the deck for roll call. Quickly the officers and staff of the ship rushed to their various stations. Reaching the deck of the ship, we discovered that Elder Larson was gathering his group of Saints on the port side of the ship. He began taking roll. As he said, "Whitman," I yelled aloud, "We're all here!" It was at that moment I realized I had received an answer to a young girl's prayer.

To my heart's delight we stayed on the deck in our

own circle of love and new beginning. My heart was brimming with gratitude. Joined by three other voices, I joyously started to sing.

> *Oh, say but I'm glad I'm glad,*
> *Oh, say but I'm glad,*
> *Jesus has come and my cup runneth o'er.*
> *Oh, say but I'm glad.*

We watched the small tugboat forge the waters before us, realizing we were on our way to America. The ports of Liverpool vanished in the blur of joyful tears when Anna said, "If only Father could be here with us, it would be perfect."

Then Mother said softly, "It is perfect, Anna. God knows the journey of the soul. We will pray for angels to surround your father and to soften his heart. God will hear our prayers. I'm sure of it."

That evening, the Saints met together upon the upper deck for evening prayers and devotions. Elder Larson invited Lucinda to play her violin and a Brother Weston to play his tabor pipe while we all sang Christmas hymns together. There is nothing quite as beautiful as listening to music while watching the waves dance. Not long after, Elder Larson excused everyone by saying, "May you all sleep well with the rocking of the ship, and Merry Christmas, everyone."

However, for a good hour, four silhouettes could be seen standing huddled against the railing. The moon was like a silver sliver, accompanied by a deep blue sky. The stars reflected upon the waves of the ocean, making it appear like an endless sheet of diamonds. I can hardly describe the beauty of that night while looking across the horizon.

Mother started to sing,

"Oh, come, all ye faithful, joyful and triumphant!"

We girls joined in and sang in loud proclamation to the world:

"O come let us adore Him,
Christ the Lord."

Holding tightly to one another, we recognized the song had an even greater meaning this Christmas.

Fresh Outlook

Fresh air seemed an unusual gift. and I found that spending so much time in the darkness of the ship rendered my spirit in search of freedom. Clear blue skies and clouds billowing before my eyes often invited prayers of thanksgiving. Too often there were mornings when I would climb onto the deck and be faced with a fearsome wind. In spite of it, I braced myself against the railing and let the wind dance through my hair. Some days Lucinda and I would stand and look across the endless horizon and talk of future dreams.

"Hillary, what do you think? Will America be as beautiful as England? I already miss the trees and rolling green hills. What do you miss?"

"I miss stretching my toes in clean white sheets at night." I giggled. "And I think back to what it was like living in the quiet seclusion of my bedroom instead of the constant creaking sounds of the ship. It makes me nervous and uneasy."

"Sometimes with the rocking of the ship, it reminds me of our mantle clock going tick, tock, tick, tock. I miss our home and our father. Hillary, what will become of him? Do you think he misses us, Hillary?" Lucinda questioned.

"I wondered if Father ever had thoughts about me. For four long years I wondered."

"Father wouldn't let us speak of you ever, but when he was gone from the house, mother, Anna, and I would pray for you. Mother hid one of your pictures in the buffet, and every Sunday we would pull it out and give you kisses. We missed you so, Hillary."

I couldn't contain my tears and wiped them away with my shawl. Breaking with the moment, I announced, "So, here we are, Lucinda—our family, bound for America."

On January 27, a sudden storm caught the Marianna by surprise. Headwinds whipped huge waves against the ship. Almost instantly I felt my stomach heave in sickness. The entire community began to fear and cry aloud. The captain called, "Batten down the hatches!" I watched with wide-eyed wonder as the crew quickly hauled in the sails. All the passengers were ordered to go below deck. I listened as the wooden battens were slammed into place. The ship began heeling heavily to the left and then right. Within a matter of minutes, we found how difficult it was to secure anything down. Buckets, crates, tins, dishes, and trunks crashed onto the floors. Children started to scream as fear found its home. Mother gathered us together upon her berth, and we offered a prayer. Cries increased, and weeping could be heard throughout the ship. I thought of Sister McGuire. I could only imagine the fear that she and her children were feeling. "Mother, I believe the McGuires could use some help with the little ones. I'll be back." I immediately set out to join her. However, with everything crashing around me, I found it difficult to make my way. When I arrived, I was truly glad that I followed the prompting.

Seeing me, Sister McGuire sighed. "Oh, Hillary girl, you're an answer to my prayers. Trying to hush the children is impossible. Even my own fears are playing with my head. Albert hasn't stopped crying for even a moment since the storm began. What will become of us, Hillary?"

I quickly plucked Albert from her arms and held him

close, bracing myself against a post. The creaking of the ship sounded even more intense in their area of the ship. My heart brushed against a memory. "Albert, I will sing for you. I taught this song to another little boy, when he was just a baby. His name is Stephen, Stephen Clark. He lives far, far away, back in England." I held Albert closer and started to sing my spinning song. It reminded me of many times I had rocked Stephen back and forth with the motion of the spinning wheel.

> *In the morning when the thread*
> *of sunlight breaks the dark*
> *I can see the glory of the Lord.*
> *As the clouds drift through the sky,*
> *in endless rippled joy*
> *I can see the glory of the Lord.*

Albert listened, and I continued to sing loud enough for Benjamin to hear as well. As I stroked Albert's hair, it brought back memories of the Clarks and the spinning wheel. I wondered if Miriam had set to spinning yet.

All of a sudden, I could hear the deep booming voice of the Captain, "Send me the Mormon leader, I need the man in charge of the Saints!" Quickly the demand rippled throughout the ship. Reaching Elder Larson, he sensed the urgency, and immediately joined the captain.

"Good man, you must pray for a miracle! Talk with your God, or we all shall be found shortly within the depths of the sea! It will be our grave, I tell you!"

Seeing the fear in the captain's face and hearing it in his voice, Elder Larson quickly gathered together a small assembly of the brethren. Unitedly, the men stood in a small circle and braced themselves as Elder Larson was the voice of the heartfelt prayer.

"Father, we need thy help! Without thy aid, we are bound to die. Please, please protect the Marianna, and all aboard, and bring peace unto the sea."

I joined with other voices in a strong, "Amen!"

Almost immediately, the ship's creaking and pitching stopped. Within moments, it was as if peace had been poured upon the decks. The ship was barely moving. A solid hush of reverence filled the ship as even the babies became quiet—so quiet that as I held Albert in my arms, he fell asleep.

"Sweet peace, Albert," I whispered. "You can sleep now and have no fear."

"That was a miracle, Hillary!" whispered Sister McGuire excitedly.

"Indeed it was, one that none of us shall ever forget." I said, breathing deeply. "God heard our prayer and answered."

The Captain was taken by wide-eyed wonder and stood in silent amazement. So stunned with the whole of it, he couldn't even utter a word. If I hadn't seen it for myself, I would have thought it impossible for him to cry. Yet I saw his eyes and the tears streaming upon his cheeks.

Elder Larson said to all within his voice, "Now, good Saints, the Lord has done his part. He has answered with a miracle. Remember this moment and write it down." Then looking around at the luggage, furniture, and clothing strewn upon the walkways, Elder Larson instructed, "Now, let's pick up the clutter of all that has fallen and get things back in godly order. As soon as you have your area tidy, then take to rest and extend some prayers of gratitude."

I returned to see my mother and sisters picking up our clothing that had fallen from the trunks. "Oh, wasn't that incredible!" I whispered. "Imagine, here we are in the middle of the wide open ocean. For hours we have been tossed to and fro. The captain felt we would all surely die."

"It was a miracle, for sure!" proclaimed Anna.

"We could have easily perished in the deep sea," said Lucinda.

Then Mother added softly, "And your father would have never known."

Mother got quiet as she folded some of the clothing and carefully repacked them. Wiping her eyes, she said, "Perhaps, girls, if we unite in prayer for your father, God will answer that prayer too. Perhaps his anger will be stilled just as much as the sea."

America!

On Thursday morning, February 6, 1840, a loud voice broke the dawn. "Land!"

Within a matter of moments, it seemed as though everyone on the ship was rushing for the stairs that led to the upper deck. It was apparent that everyone was eager to get a glimpse of America for themselves.

Elder Larson, raising his voice, insisted, "Order! We must have order. Everyone will have their moment to see. We have all waited, and we can wait just a little longer if need be. Let's be organized and move slowly, one by one toward the deck."

I welcomed the sight of land and the sounds of the seagulls. It's amazing what seven weeks upon the sea can do for one's gratitude. In all the faces I could see eager excitement, anticipation, and tears. As I stood against the ship's railing, I felt to breathe deeply of the moment. I imagined that some of the passengers would have grand reunions with their families. Elder Larson gathered his group of Saints together on the corner of the deck and gave us our parting directions. He had been a wise shepherd to the whole of us. Despite our eagerness to enter into our new life, Elder Larson asked us to join together in a prayer of thanksgiving. There upon the wooden deck, we all knelt for one final prayer together. Farewell embraces were bestowed with the reality of the parting.

"I shall meet you on the dock, Mother. I will help with little Albert and his family once more. It will only be a matter of a few moments, and then we can face America together," I said with a smile and began making my way to the McGuire's berth.

It was just as I imagined. Sister McGuire was trying to get all the children ready for departure. The children were filled with eagerness.

"I've come to help. I'll carry young Albert." Her smile showed my help was welcome. With arms full of children and luggage, we moved toward the deck.

"Oh, Hillary, thank you. Thank you for everything you have done for my family. We shall miss your stories and singing. The journey was so much easier because of you. Bless you, girl. I know it was God who brought you into our lives that day in Liverpool."

Leading the way up the steps, I once again thought about the different parting memories I had. "We shall meet someday again."

Stepping onto the platform, Sister McGuire recognized her brother and began to shout for him. The look upon her face was of pure happiness. He quickly joined us and greeted them with a quick inspection of the little ones. I imagined it was like unto a heavenly experience to see each other again after so many years apart.

"I'll be in good hands now, Hillary," said Sister McGuire, squeezing my hand. "My brother will take care of us. May God bless you in your life, as you have blessed ours."

I smiled and gave a nod and then pinched little Albert's

cheeks. "You be a good boy for your mother, and the rest of you, be good helpers always," I urged. In a matter of moments, they disappeared into the crowd.

Quickly picking up my own bag, I turned to locate my mother and sisters. It was a moment of confusing joy. On tiptoes, I scanned the sea of faces—smiling faces. I could sense the excitement in the air.

"Good sister, are you lost?" Suggested a young gentleman, looking directly into my face.

"I'm looking to find my family. My mother was wearing a green hat with a dark brown cloak." As I looked into the crowd, it seemed there were considerable green hats and brown coats. I giggled, and stepped upon a crate to get a better view.

"There they are, standing on the top of the ramp!" I said pointing. I waved hard so they could see me, as it was too noisy to render a voice loud enough.

"Let me help you, miss," he said, picking up my luggage. "Together we will push through the massive crowd. Are you one of those Mormons?" he asked.

I proudly announced, "I am a Latter-day Saint through and through!"

"I as well. I'm Elder Caitlin Fairbanks. Pleased to make your acquaintance. I'm sent to escort the Saints to the immigration processing station and then to your host families," I followed closely, not wanting to get lost in all the hustling. We finally reached the site where my family was waiting.

Tipping his hat, he greeted, "Good day to you all. I'm Elder Fairbanks, and I will help you locate your leader. We are grouping the Saints in alphabetical order. Letters A through G—"

"We're the Whitman family," my mother said with a smile.

"Elder Madsen has the Rs to Zs." Looking across the crowd, we saw a sign indicating our group.

"We must get you all checked in by the doctor. He will ensure that you are not bringing any strange disease upon our soil," he said while adding a wink of jest.

"You said your name is Caitlin? I more frequently hear it as a girl's name." I smiled.

"My parents gave me the name. My mother's name is Catherine and my father's mother was named Lynette. It's the only way that I can figure the meaning of it. I think they simply put the two together, forming Caitlin." Then he pointed north. "See the man in the black and gray suit, standing by the ship's toggled rope? That's Elder Madsen. He will help you. Perhaps we shall meet again," he said, nodding and bidding farewell.

Elder Madsen held a journal containing names of his stewardship. Mother and my sisters stood with intense anticipation.

Tears came to my eyes as I heard my mother declare, "I am Clarissa Whitman, and this is my daughter Hillary Whitman."

Then in turn, Lucinda announced her name and Anna curtsied as she said, "I'm Anna Marie Whitman." I took hold of Lucinda's hand and gave her a warm squeeze and then placed my arm around Anna's shoulder. "We're here, can you believe it, in America? All of us together!"

"Except for Father . . ." said Anna, sounding concerned.

"We will talk later about Father," said Mother, bending down to pick up the luggage. "For now, we will think of our new beginnings."

Forever Cherished

February 14, 1840

It was agreed by all that February 14, Valentine's Day, would be the perfect date for becoming members of the Church. Little did we know just how cold a day it would be. There was ice on parts of Hancock Pond, but I could only see three determined faces that morning.

"I guess it will show God how much we love him," said Anna as our teeth chattered and we stood huddled on the edge of the water.

"Now, don't slip on the rocks," I warned. "Rebecca Clark nearly drowned when she was getting baptized. She and Brother Mitchell fell into the ice cold water."

I excitedly watched as Elder Larson took my mother carefully by the hand and entered into the freezing water. Mother's face was bright red, but there was a warmth that I could see within her eyes as she smiled at me. The short baptismal prayer was offered and then Elder Larson lowered her into the water. I rushed and quickly wrapped a blanket around her body, and I could feel her body quivering.

Young Elder Fairbanks had joined with us and welcomed the opportunity to participate in the baptism. Taking Lucinda by her arm, he cautiously stepped upon the rocks. I guess my description of Rebecca's baptism made him even more careful. I stood, waiting with blankets and quilts ready. My toes were almost frozen, so I could only imagine their bodies becoming numb.

"I'm dripping in the Spirit, Hillary, just like you," smiled Lucinda as she deliberately wrapped her wet and dripping arms around me. I quickly covered her within a blanket.

"Only one more to baptize this morning," announced

Elder Larson. "Come quickly, Miss Anna, before you are taken with a chill even before you're dipped." Anna rushed into the water, and with a broad smile, she said, "I'm ready to be a Saint."

My joy, my dream, my prayers had been heard and answered. Watching my sisters and my mother baptized, it was clearly a day to be forever cherished.

"Into the buggy everyone!" exclaimed Elder Larson. "We must be quick about it. We could all freeze to death." Within a matter of minutes, three dresses were dripping beside a fire. I was stirring the soup and waiting for everyone to dress. Mother began drying Anna's long hair with a towel.

"Do you think that Father will be angry with us?" asked Anna, adding, "Now that we all are baptized?"

Mother looked directly into her eyes and held Anna's face gently. "It does not matter, Anna, what your father thinks about us being baptized. It only matters to God that we believe. Don't forget, Anna, if God can find a ship in the middle of the ocean and still the waters with a priesthood prayer, then God can do anything!"

While sipping some hot chocolate from a teacup, I noticed a small tear in Lucinda's dress, which was hanging to dry. "Lucinda, evidently you caught your dress on a rock when you were baptized. It has a tear in it. Let me stitch it for you so it is ready for the Sabbath." I gathered my sewing supplies together. I then took out my porcelain sewing thimble and placed it on my fingertip. For a moment my mind tried to visualize Miriam and the family. "Miriam gave me this thimble for Christmas."

In the bottom of the sewing box was the slip of paper with the thought she had written with the gift. "Miriam wrote this note and gave it to me with the thimble. It was my gift for Christmas. 'God can mend every broken heart, stitch any fault, and create with all power that which has infinite possibilities.' Isn't that beautiful?"

Mother came closer and held up my hand to see the thimble closer. "She loved you, Hillary, and I am so thankful to God that the Clark family was there for you. I pray that God will mend a broken heart . . . and a broken family."

"You're thinking of Father, aren't you, Mother?"

"I love him," she said firmly. "But I could not condone some of the feelings he was spreading. He was so unfair with you, and he spoke so unkindly of the Latter-day Saints. He mocked Joseph Smith, and . . ." She paused for a thought and then said, "He became so different and hardened, and it broke my heart."

Taking Lucinda's dress from my hands, she said, "Please, let me stitch the dress. I haven't sewn in weeks. And might I try your sewing thimble?" Resting in the chair by the fire, mother unwound the bobbin and drew off a piece of thread. I paused to watch her lick the thread into a fine point and thread the needle. I savored the nearly forgotten sight. My smile broadened as she began humming a familiar melody. My heart felt at home again. Mother smiled at me and shared, "Hillary, there is something within the thin threads that reminds me of the faith we must have in God. If we stitch our hearts to his, then we are allowed to see how God can weave and stitch the miracles." At that moment, I saw even deeper within my mother's soul. "Stitch away, Mother. Stitch away."

"Perhaps, Hillary, you can send them a late Valentine's card. Surely the Clark family are waiting to hear from you. They probably are wondering if you are in America.

"Yes, this is a perfect day to write a letter. They need to know I arrived in America. They will be so surprised that you sailed with me. They will be so thrilled with all of my news and happenings. I smiled as the memories cascaded through my mind. I giggled and then said aloud so my sisters would hear as well, "I think we need a cow."

"A cow?" asked Anna.

"Yes, a big cow, with black eyes as big as oranges," I grinned. "We'll have milk and chocolate cake to celebrate."

I giggled aloud and again agreed, "Yes, I need to write a letter. I am sure they are thinking me."

I drew out pages of my stationery. "I know they will be thrilled to hear of everything that has happened. Can you imagine their joy when I tell about you all surprising me on Christmas Eve? I'll tell them of our special Valentine's Day and that you've all been baptized! I have so much to say, so many stories to share—the ocean, the captain, the miracle . . ." I dipped my pen into the ink and began my journey of words.

CHAPTER VII

Someday

LUCINDA stood by the front door all fidgety and then excitedly yelled, "There's a letter for you, Hillary. It's from the Clarks. It says Sedgley on the front page." Instantly my pace increased and I felt my smile couldn't be contained. "A letter!" It had been months since I had sent my letter to them. I was beginning to wonder if it had been lost. I quickly took the letter. Recognizing her writing, I proclaimed, "It's Miriam!" Sliding a knife under the wax seal, I eagerly began reading aloud.

April 6, 1840
Dearest Hillary,

We were so thrilled to receive your letter. I could hardly wait to read it. I used your letter to motivate the children to complete their chores quickly, and it worked! I gathered everyone around the table and read it aloud. We were delighted with your generous news. I know that God is truly aware of you, Hillary.

I tried to imagine your complete surprise when your sisters and mother appeared on the ship. I couldn't help it, I cried for a good hour. I'm sure it was a joyous moment. I would give a pretty penny to have seen the sight for myself. I know it must have truly set your heart with comfort.

When you wrote about the storm on the ship, I felt the fear within the words you expressed. When you spoke of the priesthood and testified of the miracle of prayer, Andrew paid full attention. It made me reflect once again on the many prayers you offered on the

*day Stephen was born. Hillary, I miss you so. Everyone misses you.
I must share that for weeks after your departure, little Stephen cried,
"Hilly, Hilly," and everyone moped around for weeks. I was surprised when Andrew set to milking the cow again without your help
and complained, "It's not the same without Hillary."*

*I cried as you wrote about Valentine's Day and that your family
were all "dripping in the Spirit." It made me recall some of our
long, cherished talks. Remember your wish that someday your family
would understand your feelings for the gospel? Your news causes my
heart to rejoice for you. Our family prayers continue to be offered in
your behalf. Know this, Hillary, that we always include your father
in our prayers. We pray for his change of heart.*

*Millicent wants me to ask if that Elder Caitlin Fairbanks is
handsome? From your letter it sounds like he is more than just inter-
ested in performing his priesthood obligations.*

*We have set the farm on the market to sell. We are pretty firm
on a price and hope our prayers will be answered as well. I am posi-
tive that the Lord is tiring of our constant petitions. A Mr. Crawford,
from Essington, is considering purchasing it. If he is in agreement
with our price, we too will join ourselves with the Saints. Hopefully
we will meet again soon. It will be another joyous reunion.*

*I will send you a letter as soon as we know when we will be
sailing for America. I would love to meet your family.*

With affection,
Miriam

Christmas Eve 1840

"Let's sing another Christmas carol. There is nothing in
the world that brings more joy than Christmas music," I said
with a broad smile.

"This is one of my favorite songs," said Lucinda, placing the music on the wooden stand, "Coventry Carol." We

gathered together and sang to the violin's melody.

> *O sisters too, how may we do,*
> *For to preserve this day*
> *This poor youngling for whom we do sing*
> *Bye, bye, lullay, lullay.*

A loud knock upon the door interrupted our singing. Eagerly Anna opened the door and politely wished, "Good evening, and a merry Christmas."

A robust gentleman stood in the doorway. Removing his hat, he returned the greeting, "Good evening, and a merry Christmas to you, young lady. It was good to hear the music—almost sounded like angels from heaven singing." Then pausing and looking at the group, he asked, "I am in hopes that this is the Whitman home?"

"Yes, we are the Whitmans," said my mother, stepping forward.

"Whitmans from Stafford, England?" he asked with hope in his voice. We cautiously nodded our heads in the affirmative. Seeing our instant interest, he spoke quickly and reassuringly, "I am Elder John Thomas, a missionary from the Church of Jesus Christ of Latter-day Saints. I have traveled far to find you. I have been in search of your family for quite some time now."

"Looking for us?" Mother asked. "What for? Is there something wrong?"

"No, I don't believe so. I carry a message from your husband, William."

"A message?" we all chorused.

"Yes, I have a letter from William."

"Oh, excuse our manners. We haven't even asked to take your hat and coat. Clearly, you see our intense interest." Lucinda quickly took his coat and pulled a chair for him to sit upon. He then shared, "I have returned recently from a mission in England and bring you news from your husband, William." We all gathered closer.

"Is he all right? Is he well?" inquired Mother.

"Quite well, the last time I saw him."

"Does he still hate the Mormons?" asked Lucinda. "I'm sure he was mad at us for leaving."

"Hillary, get Elder Thomas some hot cider in a cup," said Mother, drawing a chair close to him. "Tell us of my William. How did you come to know him?" questioned Mother.

"Oh, I happened to be attending one of his sermons. He had invited a few of the missionaries to attend. Little did we know upon the invitation that he merely wanted us to be witnesses as he burned a Book of Mormon."

"Burned another Book of Mormon?" interrupted Anna. "Can you go to hell for doing that?"

"No, you can't go to hell for that, silly," said Lucinda, looking aghast at Anna. "Father is not going to hell."

"Does my father speak of us?" asked Anna.

"Yes, child, he speaks of all of you, and by his description, I believe you must be Anna. It's your auburn hair and freckles that gives way to discovery." Anna smiled.

Pausing for a moment, he then said, "I must share with you a few facts." Slowly he continued while getting comfortable in the chair, "Not long after you left for America, just about this same time a year ago, I believe, I was preaching to a rather large group assembled at the Hamstead farm. Your William walked into the room. There was a distinct ripple of murmuring upon his entrance. His coming was disturbing to a number in the audience and rendered them visibly uncomfortable. I later realized they had been part of his congregation. Gratefully, your William stood in the far back while we were preaching. I must admit I was a touch nervous from our previous encounter and concerned as to what he might say or do. As I spoke, I felt to speak directly to him as prompted by the Spirit. I bore testimony of the truthfulness of the gospel. At times I observed how some of the folk would look over in his direction and watch and observe him. At the conclusion of the meeting, I witnessed a few holding their heads down as they passed by him. He kindly waited until all had left the room. I realized then that he was bound to speak to us. I remember well his pointed statement that boiled with intensity, 'I have lost my entire family and flock because of you Mormons! I hate you, your church, your Joe Smith, and your golden Bible. Your preaching has lured many of my congregation away. Your book of lies has cost me dearly.' Then he stopped, and with more intensity and anger voiced, 'I cannot afford to lose anymore!'

I returned directly, "Neither can the Lord, good brother." He was upset with my quick clip and left the room in a huff. It was several weeks before I saw him again. I felt prompted and impressed to call upon him at your home. I was concerned that I had spoken in offence to his spirit.

"Clearly, Elder Thomas, that visit took a large amount of courage," I said.

"Indeed."

"Go on, Elder Thomas. What happened next?" asked Mother eagerly.

"He opened the door slowly and responded as if he were waiting for me. He simply stated, 'I thought you might come.' That was a bit of a surprise to me. Your William looked broken, his face drawn in despair. He spoke softly, 'Come in, please.' He was so different than before."

"He invited you in?" I asked.

"Yes, we stood in the hallway. Your home was in a bit of disarray—seemed so empty of life. By the looks of things, he must have been greatly upset. The spinning wheel lay broken into pieces on the floor as well as countless shards of broken dishes, and glass was scattered everywhere. William could plainly see my concern and said, 'My anger sought to destroy everything. It is by a miracle of God that I didn't burn the house down.'"

My mother gasped, "Oh, William."

"Continue, brother. What then?" I asked.

"By the dim light, I could see his eyes were red and swollen. Then he admitted to me, 'For weeks I have lived with an unrelenting anger as well as resentment. I hated everything and everyone—even God. I believe I am responsible for it all. I have lost my precious family, my congregation. Anyone of importance has abandoned my voice.'

"It was evident his heart was heavy as he shared so openly, 'For days I couldn't sleep or eat. As you can see, I haven't felt one bit like cleaning up my destruction. I have been left to ponder, and ponder long I have.' He then walked over to his desk and picked up a book. He said, 'Elder Thomas, I have burned many copies of this book. But I wanted to prove it wrong. I have read it twice.'"

"Father read the Book of Mormon?" I questioned with surprise.

"Yes, it was a bit of a surprise to me as well. Then, sweeping broken glass off of the settee, he invited me to sit. He then sadly told of how he had disowned his own daughter and sent you away," he said, looking directly at me. My heart sent a lump into my throat.

"He wept aloud as he shared, 'Four years I have lived in bitterness.' I could feel of his despair. Then he said, 'Brother Thomas, I am filled with regret. I was so puffed up in myself. I couldn't begin to see or feel what my daughter Hillary believed was true. I had no thoughts of listening to such a young girl.'"

"Oh, Father . . ." I whispered as my tears began to fall. I looked at Mother. Tears were already wetting her cheeks.

"So you can see, I believe with full heart my visit was directed by God. We talked for hours that night, and it was with the sunrise we realized the length of our discussion. There were many tears shed, and then William asked me to kneel and pray with him. After the prayer he humbly asked, 'Brother Thomas, will you baptize me?'"

"Baptized?" I asked, surprised.

"Yes. He said, 'I have a testimony of this Book of Mormon, and with this burning in my soul, I know I must be baptized.'"

Joy and disbelief filled all of our faces. Amazed with the news, we seemed to be replaying the words in our minds: "baptized," "testimony," "burning in my soul." Then, fully realizing what he had said, we began riddling Elder Thomas with questions:

"Believes the Book of Mormon?"

"Joined the Church . . ."

"He left his church?"

"Baptized?"

"What . . ."

"Where?"

Elder Thomas couldn't even begin to answer our questions, and without saying anything, he let us continue to ask question after question. Our excitement couldn't be contained.

"What happened to his congregation? Is he all right?" Mother stammered. "I can't believe it . . . This is a miracle. My William, a Latter-day Saint."

"Good family," Elder Thomas finally exclaimed while raising his arms to quiet us. "It has taken many months to find you. I realize this joyful message is a surprise gift—filled with glad tidings this very Christmas Eve."

"We must celebrate!" cheered Lucinda.

"What wonderful news. This is a glorious holiday!" Mother cried.

It was then I noticed Elder Thomas glance at the sideboard filled with some remaining food.

"Are you hungry, Elder Thomas?" I asked.

His eyes widened, accompanied with a modest grin. "I see you carry the tradition of England—even to the mince pie. Might you have some extra food for two hungry elders?"

"Two elders? Oh, excuse me, please. I was so taken with your news," said Mother, "somehow it was as though the whole world stopped. Yes, yes, of course. Have all the food you can eat."

"Oh, mercy me! I nearly forgot about my companion! He must be out tending to the needs of the horses, probably securing grass and water for them. Hillary would you please take out a lantern. I see it is getting darker by the minute."

Mother rejoiced aloud while carving the turkey, "I can't believe it! My William baptized. Praise God!"

Bring the Light

Grabbing my coat from the peg and lighting the wick to the lantern, I stepped into the cold night air. I called aloud, raising the lantern high over head while searching the horizon. I started walking to the barn. "Elder? Hello? I bring you a light for you to see. Elder, where are you?" Then I heard a soft voice speak from behind me.

"Hillary," the voice trembled as he spoke, "can you—will you—ever forgive me? I am so sorry . . ."

I instantly recognized the voice. I choked hard and for a moment held my breath. Then slowly I turned.

"Oh, Hillary, can you . . ."

I held the lantern up to see his face. "Father, oh, Father!" Resting the lantern on the ground, I rushed into his arms. My heart felt home again. I eagerly spoke, "Will I forgive you? A million times—yes!" Squeezing him so tightly, I felt like soft butter, melted in forgiveness. Joy filled my heart to overflowing. I knew that moment must be shared. "Mother! Mother! You must come quick!"

Joy to the World

Candles flickered on the Christmas tree. The fire burned brightly as the brick hearth was surrounded by a small circle of smiles.

"Let's sing another Christmas carol!" Lucinda begged.

"This is the best Christmas in all the world," Anna said, curling even more tightly in the arms of her father.

Joy to the world, the Savior reigns!
Let men their songs employ;
While fields and floods, rocks, hills and plains
Repeat the sounding joy,
Repeat the sounding joy,
Repeat, repeat, the sounding joy.

Well into the night, as Elder Thomas had found comfort in sleep, our little Whitman family of five sat around the table. It was a time of reconnecting hearts and memories.

"Remember, Mother, you told us, 'hearts can be softened and miracles can happen,' and this Christmas we have our miracle." I grinned and squeezed my father's hand tightly, looking deep into his eyes. Oh, how I missed those blue-gray, loving eyes.

"What a blessing we have—all together in heart and soul," said Mother.

"It's true," my father said solemnly, "I know that hearts can be changed. God opened my eyes to find the truth, as well as to find my family. I wish that everyone could feel so blessed as I this moment. God has granted me back my sweet, sweet angels—all of them." His voice cracking with emotion, he added, "With full heart, I am thankful to you, Hillary, for your unwavering courage. You were such a young girl with so much faith. Tonight, when you came outside with that lantern and called aloud, 'I bring you a light!'—you did. You brought more than a lantern in the darkness, you brought to this family the greatest light possible." Tears were now streaming down his cheeks. "I am so sorry. To imagine all those days and years without you—"

"Shhh! Father," I whispered, "I'm filled to overflowing. There is no room for regrets or sadness. I have dreamed and prayed so often for this moment. This night is far better than I ever imagined possible. It's perfect."

With a large smile upon his face, my father stepped away from the table. Opening his travel bag, he reached deep and pulled forth a book. "Look familiar?" Placing it in the center of the table, with tears accompanying his voice, he spoke meekly, "I believe it is God who lifted the blindness from my eyes so that I could see all the possibilities of truth. I am filled with an overwhelming sense of joy. I had let bitterness, fear, ego, and pride stand in the way of God's work. It took losing my family to get my attention." Focused on everyone gathered around the table, he shared, "I shall never forget that day in December as I walked through the front door of our home. It was filled with an uncommon quiet. Gone were the sounds of the spinning wheel. It had been whirling round for weeks and weeks. Sounds of Lucinda practicing her violin had disappeared. All of our common daily chatter was absent. A Christmas garland hung on the fireplace, wreaths were tied to the windows—it all looked well enough. Yet shortly I found everything—closet, drawers, baskets—empty. All that remained was the sound of the mantle clock ticking." Then glancing over at my mother, he said, "I saw the letter that you placed on the dining table—just one letter, after twenty-two years of marriage. Two sentences stood out boldly and were enough to season my anger:

"'We will join ourselves with the Latter-day Saints. We are going to Zion.'

"I screamed aloud, 'Zion!' I spun around the room and found I had so much hatred and bitterness in my heart that I broke every dish I could lay my hands upon. The floor was covered with bits of broken glass. I threw the spinning wheel against the wall. It broke into pieces. Sober truths that in all reality my family was in pieces as well."

Mother's eyes welled up with tears, and she wrinkled her brow in hopes of containing her pain. Lucinda, Anna, and I were fixed upon listening.

"I felt such hostility within. Never before had I felt such a surge of hot anger. Inner voices constantly urged me to harbor an attitude of contempt. It seemed I was powerless against those feelings and was surrounded with a consuming sense of unrelenting darkness. For days I just sat in the parlor, staring out the window. I let anguish and animosity seep into my soul as I festered in pain." Father breathed deeply and then continued on. "After much discontent and fret, I found myself utterly exhausted. Those who mattered most to me were gone. I didn't want anyone to know you had left me, and had left me for that church and your so-called Zion. I was too proud to ask after you. I then developed anger toward God in allowing this to happen. I could no longer stand before a congregation. I drew the conclusion that I had no further purpose or reason to live. I might as well die. I was resigned to just fade away."

We all sat silent and spellbound as Father continued, "Exhausted, I crawled into bed. Resting my head upon the pillow I felt something hard beneath it."

Father then reached for the book lying upon the table and held it to his chest. "This book, this very book." His voice was filled with silent emotion. He could not speak. Yet it was apparent that he was filled with powerful and profound feelings. He wept.

Looking across the table to Mother, I exchanged a knowing grin with her. With a warm smile and a wink, Mother replied, "Well, it worked once before, Hillary Whitman. Sometimes all one needs to do—is sleep on it."

I felt like rejoicing and started to sing. I could see everyone's instant delight and was quickly joined by all.

> *"Oh, say but I'm glad, I'm glad.*
> *Jesus has come and my cup runneth o'er,*
> *Oh, say but I'm glad.*
> *Wonderful, marvelous things he brings . . .*

I thought of all the prayers that had been extended and all the tears that had been shed. My dream had come true. We were all together again, and it was just as I imagined it would be.

Gazing at the stars that night, I blew a kiss to God for hearing prayers and answering them. It was a perfect Christmas. Joy was mine once again as I heard my father express, "Merry Christmas, my sweet, sweet angels."

ABOUT THE AUTHOR

 RADUATING from Brigham Young University with a degree in speech and drama has provided Shauna V. Brown with many opportunities to write and direct original plays and presentations for Church and community groups. Over the past fifteen years, she has shared her musical talents and original scripts for LDS pioneer trek groups now numbering in the hundreds. Shauna has also enjoyed being a presenter at BYU Education Week and Women's Conferences.

Shauna and her husband, Rick, have been blessed with six children (lovingly known as Brown's Sunshine Factory). Shauna considers it an additional blessing to be generating other sunshine outlets. At the time of publication, a dozen grandchildren add to the sunshine. For the past twenty years, Shauna has written an original Christmas story each year as a gift to neighbors and friends.